CW00869876

HOMEMADE
FAMILY MEALS

HOMEMADE FAMILY MEALS

Caroline Barty

Bridget Jones

Liz Wolf-Cohen

Photography by Ian Garlick

MQP

Published by MQ Publications Ltd
12 the Ivories
6–8 Northampton Street
London N1 2HY
Tel: 020 7359 2244
Fax: 020 7359 1616
E-mail: mail@mqpublications.com
www.mqpublications.com

North American office
49 West 24th Street
8th Floor
New York, NY 10010
E-mail: information@mqpublicationsus.com

Copyright © 2006 MQ Publications Limited
Recipes: Caroline Barty, Bridget Jones, Liz Wolf-Cohen
Photography: Ian Garlick
Home Economy: Felicity Barnum-Bobb
Illustrations: Penny Brown

ISBN: 1-84601-142-6
978-1-84601-142-9

1 3 5 7 9 0 8 6 4 2

All rights reserved. No part of this publication may be reproduced or transmitted
in any form or by any means, electronic or mechanical, including photocopy,
recording, or any information storage and retrieval system now known or to be
invented without permission in writing from the publishers.

Printed in China

IMPORTANT: Those who might be at risk from the effects of salmonella
poisoning (the elderly, pregnant women, young children and those suffering
from immune deficiency diseases) should consult their GP with any concerns
about eating raw eggs.

Contents

Introduction   6

1 Poultry   16

2 Meat   50

3 Fish & Shellfish   90

4 Vegetarian   124

5 Salads & Side Dishes   160

6 Desserts   212

Menu Ideas   248

Index   252

Introduction

Surrounded by fast-food franchises, meals on the run and off-the-shelf prepared meals, the mention of "homemade" when referring to food conjures up the image of a dish that is nutritious, freshly made with quality ingredients, by hand, and not delivered off a factory conveyor belt.

Think back to the time of your grandmother when all meals were "homemade." In just a few decades our eating habits have been turned on their head and we have become dependent on convenience foods and burgers from the drive-thru windows. In our eagerness to pack more into our lives, and for families where both parents work, the desire to give up less time to cooking has become the norm. However, we relish the taste of "homemade" food when we have been invited to a meal where the table is groaning with a crispy roast chicken, hand-cut fries, and a traditional apple pie.

The exponential rise of prepared meals in supermarket cases means that we are cooking less and less and losing basic cooking skills. This in turn makes us hesitant, insecure cooks who will scurry off to pick up a takeout or add a jar of prepared sauce to a plate of spaghetti rather than struggle to make a dish that may or may not work out. We are opting for the convenience of having a meal that requires no more effort than switching on the oven or moving a package from the freezer to the microwave. There is a great deal to be said for the speed in which a meal can be served up—there are occasions when it is the perfect solution to a long day or to the unexpected arrival of four extra teenage mouths to fill, or to a sports event on the television that cannot be interrupted. But we all know that it never tastes as good as when you make it yourself, and that most often it contains more fat, salt, sugar, and flavor enhancers than is good for us.

Homemade Meals shows us that cooking doesn't have to be a chore, that meals needn't take a lifetime to prepare, and that we don't have to be a superchef to make a tasty, wholesome dish. Remember too, that homemade meals do not have to look as if they have been restaurant made. That's not homemade! A dish can look a little rough around the edges and still be delicious. Homemade is going for second helpings!

Each recipe in the first four chapters of this book is part of a menu. On each recipe you will find a menu suggestion. So if you fancy a Tuna Noodle Casserole then you can complete the meal with the rest of the dishes on the menu. For quick reference you can consult the Menu Ideas on page 248. The menus are a guideline only, offering a balance of daily food requirements, tastes and textures, and time management. Choose the main dish as your starting point and then consider dishes that will complement and highlight individual qualities of the different ingredients. Use your personal preferences as a guide.

Equipment

KNIVES & OTHER CUTTING EQUIPMENT

A good sharp knife that is comfortable to hold is the most essential tool in the kitchen. There is nothing worse than having to hack vegetables and saw your way through meat. Knives should be kept razor sharp. To help preserve their cutting edge, always chop on a wooden board or plastic board. Do not store your knives in silverware drawers—the edges get dulled and it is dangerous when someone reaches in. Keep them slotted individually in a wooden knife block.

Chopping knife

To chop vegetables and herbs you will need a well-balanced, general purpose cook's knife that tapers to a pointed tip.

Knife for slicing

For slicing bread you will need a knife with a long blade with hollow-ground serrations; for slicing cold meats use a knife with a long and narrow blade with good flexibility; for slicing fruit and vegetables use a small serrated knife.

Paring & peeling knife

Use these to peel and slice your vegetables. The blade of a paring knife should always be sharp.

Carving knife

This has a long, narrow blade for slicing hot, cooked meats, and is often used with a double-pronged fork to keep the meat steady.

Boning knife

This knife has a curved blade and a sharp end which can tunnel through meat easily. It's not suitable for any other job.

Filleting knife

This is the only knife to use when you have a fish to fillet. Its long, flexible blade is perfectly equipped to separate delicate flesh from bones.

Poultry shears

These heavy-duty scissors, which have one serrated blade, can easily cut through bone and cartilage.

Grater

Choose a box-shaped grater that will sit squarely on a cutting board without shifting as you grate. Each side should have a different grating surface so you can grate a variety of food textures from soft (cheese) to very hard (nutmeg).

OTHER EQUIPMENT

Pans

A set of three or four saucepans is probably sufficient for most households. The size of your pans depends on how many people on average you are catering for. Buy pans that have a thick and heavy gauge metal on the bottom with lids that give a tight seal. Handles should be strong and comfortable to hold and preferably heat insulated. Nonstick surfaces are fabulous for heating milk and cooking eggs and fish where almost no fat is required for cooking.

Wok

This is a very inexpensive and versatile addition to your kitchen equipment. The most useful wok that comes with a fitting lid is 14 inches in diameter. After cooking, wash the wok with hot soapy water and a brush and dry thoroughly, then momentarily place it over a hot flame. To prevent rusting, lightly wipe the inside with a little vegetable oil.

Skillets & griddle pans

Choose a heavy-bottomed, nonstick skillet for even cooking. A griddle pan is useful for searing meat, fish, and vegetables—the best griddle pans have deep ridges so the meat can sit above its fat.

Roasting pans

Stainless steel roasting pans are probably the best. Heavier ones will not scorch on the bottom when used on the top of the stove. Select one that best fits the contours of your oven. Similarly, make sure the pan is the correct size for the quantities in which you usually cook. The sides should be low enough for heat to access the surface of the food, but deep enough to hold rendered fats and juices. A rack may be placed in the pan, allowing for even roasting and for juices and fat to drip away.

Casserole dishes

Enamelled cast iron and clad metal casseroles are best because they conduct heat evenly. Make sure you have one with a tight-fitting lid.

Garlic press

Choose a sturdy aluminum or stainless steel press with a coarse mesh. Remember, crushed garlic from a press is more potent in flavor than chopped garlic. The good thing about a press is that you don't have to peel the garlic segments.

Pestle & mortar

If you want to crush herbs and spices to release their rich aromas, a solid, heavy pestle and mortar do the best job.

Strainers & colanders

Round-framed stainless steel strainers are preferable to the wire or plastic mesh variety. Stainless steel does not stain or corrode. Colanders are particularly useful for draining pasta and vegetables.

BOARDS

A big, solid wooden cutting board is your kitchen's best friend. Make sure you keep your board scrupulously clean, washing thoroughly with

detergent between ingredients to avoid cross-contamination. Buy the best board you can afford and it'll last for years. If you are particularly concerned about hygiene, you could have color-coded plastic chopping boards. Keep green for chopping vegetables, red for meat, blue for fish, and the others for cooked foods. A mezzaluna or "half moon" implement makes chopping herbs a breeze. Simply rock the blade to and fro across the special curved chopping board.

WHISKS
Balloon whisk

The classic whisk can be used for aerating both light and heavy ingredients. It's especially good for cream and butter sauces.

Egg whisk

This has more wires than an ordinary balloon whisk making it good for aerating egg-based sauces and egg whites for meringues.

BOWLS
Ceramic bowl

A traditional bowl finished with a white glaze is comfortable and easy to handle.

Glass bowl

This is a good general mixing bowl, suitable for all ingredients and heavy enough to sit firmly on the work top.

Melamine bowl

Practical, cheap and unbreakable, plastic-based bowls often have a non-slip rubber base.

Stainless steel bowl

Stainless steel is ideal for all food preparation as it is resistant to food acids and colors.

BLENDERS & FOOD PROCESSORS

Food processors are extremely versatile—they can chop, mince, purée, shred, and slice many ingredients. Blenders are good for liquefying food to make soups, sauces, and purées.

MEASURING CUPS/SPOONS
Level off ingredients in the spoons or cups for accuracy.

Staples

We are all too familiar with cupboards full of items that have been there for several years. Clear out anything that has been open for more than six months—many items should be tossed within just weeks of opening. If you are cooking for few, buy little. It may appear to be uneconomical to purchase small amounts but it is just the other side of the coin to throw away larger quantities that have been cheaper buys.

Fresh over frozen

Whenever possible buy fresh and in season and if you can, try to buy local. That way you will be able to savor new season tastes and choose recipes that reflect the passing months.

GRAINS, BEANS & PASTA

Grains

Grains are the edible seeds of grasses. Whether you are shopping for barley, bulgur wheat, cornmeal, oatmeal, or wheat, make sure you buy it fresh. The grain should be dry, plump, and even in color.

- *Oats*
- *Barley*
- *Cornmeal*
- *Bulgur or cracked wheat*
- *Arborio rice*
- *Long-grain white rice*
- *Brown rice*
- *Wild rice*
- *Basmati rice*
- *Couscous*

Beans

Beans are extremely nutritious. They are low in fat and sodium and high in fiber.

- *Red split lentils*
- *Green and brown lentils*
- *White kidney*
- *Pinto beans*
- *Cannellini beans*
- *Garbanzos*
- *Butter beans*
- *Black-eyed peas*

Pasta

Pasta can be made just with flour and water, or with eggs too. The best commercially bought pasta is marked "100% whole durum" or "pure semolina" and comes from southern Italy. Different types of pasta suit different types of sauce—thick, creamy sauces are best with chunky shapes such as penne or fusilli. Oil-based sauces suit fine pastas such as spaghetti, and chunky meat sauces are best cooked in lasagne or cannelloni. Asian noodles are mainly made from wheat, rice, buckwheat, or mung beans. The most popular are rice noodles and egg noodles.

- *Spaghetti*
- *Tagliatelle*
- *Macaroni*
- *Fusilli*
- *Farfalle*
- *Cannelloni*
- *Lasagne*

SEASONINGS

Salt

Keep a small bowl of coarse salt near the stove. Sea salt and kosher salt are highly favored in cooking and flavoring because of the absence of additives and chemicals. Generally it is in the form of larger flakes or crystals so keep a special mill for grinding.

- *Sea salt*
- *Sel gris*
- *Kosher salt*
- *Common salt*
- *Iodized salt*
- *Rock salt*
- *Seasoned salt*

Pepper

Pepper is one of the most versatile spices—not only does it add its own distinctive flavoring, but it also helps to enhance other flavors. Chili powder is a blended spice that may also contain paprika, cayenne, black pepper, and salt.

- *Black peppercorns*
- *White peppercorns*
- *Green peppercorns*
- *Ground red chile*
- *Chili powder*
- *Cayenne pepper*
- *Paprika*
- *Dried red pepper flakes*

Mustard

Mustard has been a popular condiment for thousands of years. The hot taste is released when crushed mustard seeds are mixed with liquid. English mustard is one of the hottest; Dijon is blended with wine or vinegar to give it its distinctive taste.

- *Dijon*
- *Whole-grain*
- *English*
- *American*

Vinegar

Vinegar is a by-product of wine-making, hence the different varieties such as cider and wine vinegar. Balsamic vinegar is sweeter, richer, and darker.

- *Wine vinegar*
- *Cider vinegar*
- *Malt vinegar*
- *Balsamic vinegar*
- *Flavored vinegar*

Sauces & condiments

There are so many sauces and condiments you can buy that you should try to keep a variety of them in your cupboard—that way you will always have one to complement any meal.

- *Tomato ketchup*
- *Tomato paste*
- *Sweet chili sauce*
- *Mayonnaise*
- *Red currant jelly*
- *Hoisin sauce*
- *Fruit preserves*
- *Chutney*
- *Tabasco or other hot sauce*
- *Fish sauce* is a strong, salty liquid, very popular in Southeast Asia.
- *Soy sauce* is one of the most important ingredients in Chinese cookery and comes in light and dark, the dark being the stronger, sweeter variety.
- *Worcestershire sauce* is made from, amongst others, tamarind, molasses, anchovies, soy sauce, onions, sugar, and lime.

Herbs

Five herbs that have delicate leaves and are best when they have just been picked are basil, chervil, mint, parsley, and tarragon. They are at their optimum flavor raw. Robust herbs such as bay leaf, marjoram, oregano, rosemary, and sage can withstand higher cooking temperatures.

Bouquet garni is, at its simplest, parsley, thyme, and bay leaf tied together with string, but can just be a bunch of herbs of your choice.

- *Parsley*
- *Chives*
- *Tarragon*
- *Dill*
- *Bay leaves*
- *Thyme*
- *Mint*
- *Marjoram*
- *Oregano*
- *Rosemary*
- *Sage*
- *Cilantro*
- *Basil*
- *Fennel*

Spices

Buy in small quantities and whenever possible use whole spices. This is where your pestle and mortar comes in handy.

- *Clove*
- *Cinnamon*
- *Allspice*
- *Cardamom*
- *Cumin*
- *Ginger*
- *Turmeric*
- *Saffron*
- *Caraway seeds*
- *Curry powder*
- *Vanilla*
- *Coriander*
- *Mace*
- *Garam masala*
- *Ras al hanout*

Nuts & seeds

Nuts are very nutritious, containing many vitamins and minerals, but are also high in fat. It is best to buy them still in their shell as they keep better this way. Keep nuts and seeds in an airtight container in a cool, dark place.

- *Hazelnuts*
- *Pine nuts*
- *Cashews*
- *Almonds (blanched, flaked, and ground)*
- *Brazil nuts*
- *Pistachios*
- *Walnuts*
- *Pecans*
- *Sesame seeds*
- *Sunflower seeds*
- *Poppy seeds*
- *Pumpkin seeds*

OILS

Unrefined oils are those that have been cold pressed and left to mature for a few months before bottling. They tend to be cloudy and flavorsome.

Refined oils have been extracted by modern mechanical methods. They have been treated for extended shelf life and clarity.

Virgin olive oil is useful for salads and other dishes where the fruity flavor of the oil can be savored. Mediterranean dishes benefit from the use of olive oil. Olive oil is not normally used for deep frying.

Peanut oil is a good replacement for olive oil when used for frying as it has very little smell and no flavor that will interfere with the taste of the food being prepared.

Corn oil is one of the most economical oils for shallow and deep frying, having one of the highest smoke points.

Safflower oil is very light and is recommended for use in cholesterol-lowering diets.

Walnut oil is an excellent addition to salads especially spinach. It does not keep well and it is recommended to buy small quantities.

Vegetable oils are a blend of various vegetable products—soybean, coconut, palm, cottonseed, and canola. They are good for frying because of their high smoke point.

Palm and coconut oil are high in saturated fats and should be avoided by those on low-cholesterol diets.

Flavored oils are good in salad dressings. Make your own by adding herbs, spices, and citrus zests to good olive oil and leaving it to steep for a month.

BAKING

Sugar

Natural brown sugars come from raw sugar cane that retain some of the flavor and goodness of the cane; white sugars contain no protein, vitamins, or minerals. Molasses sugar is soft, strong-flavored and very moist—good for gingerbread, fudge, and fruit cakes. Coarse sugar is gritty with large granules.

- *Granulated sugar*
- *Superfine sugar*
- *Confectioners' sugar*
- *Brown sugar*
- *Golden syrup*
- *Corn syrup (light & dark)*
- *Molasses and black treacle*
- *Turbinado sugar*

Flour

The most-used flours are made from wheat, but there is also flour made of rice, rye, buckwheat, corn, and potato. Keep flour in an airtight container in a cool, dark, dry place.

- *All-purpose flour*
- *Self-rising flour*
- *Bread flour*
- *Cake flour*
- *Whole-wheat flour*
- *Cornmeal*

Leavening agents

Always keep the essential leavenings in your cupboard as they are used extensively in baking.

- *Dry yeast*
- *Baking powder*
- *Baking soda*

Fats

Useful for cooking and baking, butter is also the base of many sauces.

- *Salted butter*
- *Margarine*
- *Unsalted butter*
- *Shortening*

Cream & yogurt

A thick, rich cream complements many a pie while yogurt is particularly good added to cooked dishes.

- *Single cream*
- *Whipping Cream*
- *Crème fraîche*
- *Heavy cream*
- *Soured cream*
- *Plain yogurt*

MISCELLANEOUS ITEMS

- *Bouillon cubes*
- *Dark and golden raisins*
- *Garlic*
- *Honey*
- *Coconut cream*
- *Gelatin*
- *Dried mushrooms*
- *Olives*
- *Capers*

COOKING METHODS

You do not have to be a trained chef to turn out a tasty meal. Practice makes perfect, and the more dishes you try, the more confident you will become. If you are an absolute beginner choose the easy options—soups and casseroles which are hard to get wrong. Read the recipe carefully before you begin to ensure that you have all the necessary ingredients (ingredient substitutes midway through preparation are not advised until you feel that you are a secure cook who has an understanding of how ingredients function and interact with other ingredients).

A few points for a healthy & happy kitchen

Make your kitchen environment an enjoyable place to be in. Keep it clean and clutter free. It is difficult to be a relaxed cook if you are constantly hunting for lost or mislaid tools and ingredients. Try to be organized—have your ingredients measured out and at hand and follow the guidelines below to make your kitchen a safer place.

- Always wash your hands with soap before and after handling food. Rinse well.
- Keep cuts and scrapes covered with a waterproof dressing.
- Always wash food. Soak fruit and vegetables for a few minutes in a bowl of clean water then rinse under a running tap.
- Wash raw poultry under running water and then pat dry with paper towels.
- Thoroughly clean all surfaces that have come in contact with raw poultry.
- Keep separate cutting boards for raw meat, fish, poultry, and vegetables. Buy a set of colored boards—red for meat, pink for poultry, blue for fish, green for vegetables. It makes life much simpler.
- Wash kitchen utensils between preparing raw and cooked foods.
- Keep dish towels clean and change frequently.
- Once food is cooked do not leave unrefrigerated for too long and never cover cooling food.
- Never re-heat food more than once. Make sure that it is piping hot all the way through.
- Store perishable foods at the correct temperature.
- Keep all refrigerated food covered and wipe up spills immediately with paper towels.
- Store raw meat, poultry and fish at the bottom of the refrigerator so that blood or moisture does not drip on other foods. This prevents bacterial cross-contamination.
- Thoroughly clean your refrigerator using a special anti-bacterial refrigerator cleaner.

POULTRY

- Spiced Chicken Pilaf with Dried Fruit & Nuts
- Spicy Chicken Kabobs
- Stir-fried Chicken with Chiles & Sweet Basil
- Chicken Satay Skewers with Sweet Chili Sauce
- Southern Fried Chicken
- Spicy Chicken Enchiladas
- Club Sandwiches
- Stuffed Cabbage Leaves
- Chicken Hunter-style
- Chicken & Sausage Gumbo
- Honey-orange Chicken
- Chicken Kiev
- Roast Stuffed Chicken
- Grilled Spiced Chicken
- Chicken & Vegetable Pie
- Spicy Peanut Chicken Noodles
- Chicken Tikka
- Lemon Chicken with Herb Tagliatelle
- Spicy Chicken Sausages
- Apple & Ginger Turkey Sandwiches
- Roast Turkey with Sausage & Sage Stuffing
- Spicy Turkey Meatballs
- Turkey-stuffed Peppers

CHAPTER ONE

POULTRY

Spiced Chicken Pilaf
with Dried Fruit & Nuts

Serves 4

¹/₃ stick (3 tablespoons) butter
6 green cardamom pods, lightly
   crushed
1 cinnamon stick
2 bay leaves
1 cup basmati rice
1¹/₂ cups chicken broth
1 tablespoon vegetable oil
1 medium onion, finely chopped
2 tablespoons flaked almonds
2 tablespoons pistachio nuts, shelled
   and roughly chopped
¹/₃ cup dried figs, roughly chopped
4–5 dried apricots, roughly chopped
6 ounces boneless chicken breast,
   skinned and cut into chunks
3 tablespoons chopped fresh cilantro
Salt and freshly ground black pepper

1 Melt half the butter in a saucepan or casserole with a tight-fitting lid. Add the cardamom pods and cinnamon stick and cook for about 30 seconds before adding the bay leaves and rice. Stir well to coat the rice in the butter and add the broth. Bring to a boil, cover tightly and reduce the heat to low. Cook very gently for 15 minutes. Remove from the heat and let stand for 5 minutes.

2 Heat the remaining butter and vegetable oil in a wok or skillet. When hot, add the onion and nuts. Stir-fry for 3–4 minutes until the nuts are beginning to brown.

3 Reduce the heat slightly and add the figs, apricots, and chicken and continue to stir-fry for a further 7–8 minutes, or until the chicken is cooked through.

4 Remove from the heat and add the hot cooked rice and chopped cilantro. Stir together well. Season to taste and serve hot.

Menu

Spiced Chicken Pilaf
with Dried Fruit &
Nuts
~
Spinach with Paneer
(p.151)
~
Tropical Fruit Salad
(p.221)

Spicy Chicken Kabobs

Serves 4

4 skinless, boneless chicken breast
fillets
2 tablespoons olive oil
1 tablespoon ground cilantro
1 tablespoon ground cumin
1 teaspoon ground turmeric
1 teaspoon ground red chile
Salt and freshly ground black pepper
4 pita breads
4 handfuls of shredded iceberg lettuce
2 tomatoes, sliced
1 small red onion, thinly sliced
Small handful of fresh cilantro leaves

For the dressing
²/₃ cup plain yogurt
2 tablespoons chopped fresh mint

1 Soak 8 wooden skewers in water for 30 minutes. Cut the chicken breast fillets into large chunks and place in a bowl. Mix the oil, ground cilantro, cumin, turmeric, and red chile together in a large bowl, and season with salt and pepper. Pour over the chicken and mix well, then thread the chicken onto the soaked skewers.

2 Heat a griddle pan until very hot and lay the skewers on it. Cook for about 10 minutes, turning the skewers occasionally, until the chicken is cooked through. Meanwhile, warm the pita breads in a low oven, then cut a slit along one side to make them into pockets.

3 To make the dressing, mix the yogurt and mint together, then season to taste.

4 Fill the pita breads with lettuce, tomato, and sliced onion. Remove the cooked chicken from the skewers and pile into the pita breads. Drizzle with the dressing and serve.

Menu

Spicy Chicken Kabobs
~
Classic Healthy Coleslaw
(p.191)
~
Meringues with Cream & Blueberries
(p.223)

Stir-fried Chicken
with Chiles & Sweet Basil

Serves 2

1 tablespoon vegetable oil

2 chicken breast fillets, thinly sliced

2 cloves garlic, crushed

2 large, fresh, red hot chiles, seeded
and sliced

$^1/_2$ onion, cut into 1-inch chunks

3 tablespoons Thai fish sauce

1 tablespoon dark soy sauce

1 tablespoon brown sugar

$^1/_4$ cup sweet fresh basil leaves

Steamed rice, to serve

Tip
Before starting any stir-fry recipe, be sure to have all the ingredients prepared—once you have started cooking there will be no time for ingredient preparation.

Menu

*Stir-fried Chicken
with Chiles &
Sweet Basil*

~

*Stir-fried Greens
with Shiitake
Mushrooms (p.179)*

~

*Lychees with Orange
& Ginger (p.229)*

1 Heat a wok over a high heat until smoking. Add the oil and then the chicken, garlic, and chiles. Stir-fry for 1 minute, then add the onion. Continue stir-frying for 5 minutes, or until the chicken is cooked through.

2 Pour in the fish sauce and soy sauce, and sprinkle over the sugar. Bring to a boil and scatter with sweet basil. Serve immediately with steamed rice.

Chicken Satay Skewers
with Sweet Chili Sauce

Serves 8

2 skinless, boneless chicken breasts
1 tablespoon chunky peanut butter
1 tablespoon soy sauce
Pinch of ground red chile
$1/3$ cup hot water
Sweet chili sauce and cucumber sticks
   to serve

Menu

*Chicken Satay
Skewers with Sweet
Chili Sauce*

~

*Rice Vermicelli with
Pork & Vegetables
(p.63)*

~

*Chilled Tangerine &
Lemon Mousse (p.233)*

1 Soak 16 bamboo skewers in cold water for at least 20 minutes. Cut each chicken breast fillet lengthwise into 8 long strips and thread each one on to a soaked skewer. Set aside.

2 Put the peanut butter in a small saucepan with the soy sauce, ground red chile, and the hot water. Stir over gentle heat, allowing the sauce to bubble until it has thickened slightly.

3 Preheat the broiler. Brush the satay sauce all over the chicken and place the skewers on a baking sheet. Broil for 8-10 minutes, turning occasionally, until the chicken is cooked through. Serve hot or warm with sweet chili dipping sauce and cucumber sticks.

Southern Fried Chicken

Makes 8

8 chicken thighs or drumsticks
2$\frac{1}{2}$ cups milk
1 tablespoon Tabasco or other hot
  sauce
1 cup all-purpose flour
1 teaspoon ground black pepper
1 teaspoon cayenne pepper
$\frac{1}{4}$ teaspoon salt
1 egg, beaten
2 cups shortening

1 Put the chicken pieces in a large saucepan in a single layer. Add the milk and hot sauce and marinate in the refrigerator for at least 2 hours.

2 Mix the flour, pepper, cayenne pepper, and salt together in a bowl.

3 Put the pan with the marinated chicken on the stovetop. Bring the milk to a boil, then reduce the heat and simmer for 20 minutes. Drain well, then pat dry and let cool for 20 minutes.

4 Dip the chicken pieces first in the seasoned flour, then the egg, and then in the flour again.

5 Heat the vegetable fat in a large skillet until very hot. Add the chicken and cook for 4-5 minutes until golden brown. Drain on paper towels before serving.

Menu

Southern Fried Chicken
~
*Chef's Salad
(p.197)*
~
*Berry Frozen Treats
(p.214)*

Spicy Chicken Enchiladas

Serves 4

Two 6-ounce jars prepared *mole poblano* paste
3 tablespoons peanut butter
1 cup chicken broth
Eight 8-inch corn tortillas
2²/₃ cups cooked, shredded Grilled Spiced Chicken (p. 37)
Salt and freshly ground black pepper
1 small onion, finely chopped
2 cups grated cheddar cheese
Sour cream and refried beans, to serve

1 Preheat a gas-fired grill to medium indirect heat.

2 Mix the *mole poblano* paste and peanut butter together in a medium saucepan over low heat. Mash together until melted. Gradually add enough of the chicken broth to make a smooth, thick sauce.

3 Warm the corn tortillas by wrapping them in aluminum foil and putting them on the grill for 3–4 minutes.

4 Spread about a quarter of the mole sauce in the bottom of a large size aluminum foil tray (13 x 6 inches). Lay one tortilla on a plate and top with about ⅓ cup shredded chicken. Season lightly with salt and pepper and sprinkle over a little of the onion, then some of the cheese. Roll up and place, seam-side down, in the aluminum foil tray. Repeat with the remaining tortillas and filling ingredients, reserving about ½ cup of the cheese.

5 Spoon the remaining *mole* sauce over the enchiladas and sprinkle with the reserved cheese. Cover the tray loosely with aluminum foil and transfer to the grill.

6 Cook for 15 minutes until the enchiladas are heated through and the sauce is bubbling.

7 Transfer the enchiladas to serving plates and drizzle each with a little sour cream. Serve immediately with a spoonful of refried beans.

Menu

Spicy Chicken Enchiladas
~
Caesar Salad (p.194)
~
Grilled Corn-on-the-Cob with Flavored Butter (p.174)

Club Sandwiches

Serves 6

18 slices white bread
3 large tomatoes, thinly sliced
3 cooked chicken breasts, thinly sliced
Salt and freshly ground black pepper
6 tablespoons mayonnaise, preferably
  homemade
18 slices lean bacon, fried until crisp
Crisp lettuce leaves

Menu

Club Sandwiches
~
*Old-fashioned
English Chips (p.164)*
~
*Caramel Ice Cream
(p.217)*

Tip

Make sure you eat
your freshly made club
sandwich straight away to
prevent your toasted bread
from getting soggy with
the mayonnaise.

1 Lightly toast the bread. Lay 6 pieces on a board and top each one with the tomato slices. Pile the sliced chicken on top and season with salt and freshly ground pepper.

2 Put a second piece of toast over the chicken and spread with the mayonnaise. Lay 3 slices of bacon on top of each one and arrange some lettuce leaves over the bacon.

3 Top with the remaining toast, halve the sandwiches diagonally and secure with toothpicks.

Stuffed Cabbage Leaves

Serves 4

8 large leaves of a dark variety of
    cabbage, such as Savoy
1 tablespoon sunflower oil
1 bay leaf
2 large onions, chopped
2 carrots, chopped
3 cloves garlic, crushed
14-ounce can chopped tomatoes
1⅓ cups chicken broth
1⅓ cups red wine
Salt and freshly ground black pepper
1 pound chicken meat, chopped
6 tablespoons fresh bread crumbs
2 tablespoons chopped fresh parsley
2 tablespoons chopped fresh sage
1 teaspoon dried oregano

1 Cut out the hard stalk at the base of the cabbage leaves. Bring a large pan of water to a boil. Add the cabbage leaves and bring back to a boil, then cook for 30 seconds, or until the leaves are softened. Pour the leaves into a colander and set aside to drain. Return the pan to the heat and add the oil, bay leaf, onions, carrots, and garlic. Stir, then cook gently for 10 minutes, or until the onions have softened slightly. Transfer half the mixture to a bowl, leaving the bay leaf in the pan, and reserve this for the stuffing.

2 Add the tomatoes, broth, and wine to the pan. Bring to a boil. Reduce the heat. Cook for 15 minutes, stirring occasionally.

3 Preheat the oven to 350°F. Add the chicken, bread crumbs, parsley, sage, and oregano to the reserved onion mixture. Season and stir until the ingredients are well combined. Press the mixture with the back of the spoon so that it binds, then divide it into 8 portions.

4 Dry the cabbage leaves on a clean dish towel. Lay each leaf down with the side with protruding veins uppermost. Put some chicken mixture slightly off-center, nearer to the stalk end of the leaf. Fold the stalk end over the filling, then fold the sides up and roll up into a parcel. Put the leaves in a deep ovenproof dish with the end of the parcel down.

5 Stir the sauce, season if necessary, and ladle it over the cabbage leaves. Cover and cook in the oven for 45 minutes, or until the leaves are tender and the filling is cooked through.

> ### Menu
>
> *Stuffed
> Cabbage Leaves*
> ~
> *Broccoli Pilaf
> (p.205)*
> ~
> *Chocolate Mousse
> (p.232)*

Chicken Hunter-style

Serves 4–6

1/3 cup all-purpose flour
Salt and freshly ground black pepper
2 1/2 pounds chicken pieces
3–4 tablespoons vegetable oil
1 onion, sliced
1 pound mushrooms, sliced
1 clove garlic, crushed
1/4 cup dry white wine
1/4 cup chicken broth or water
14-ounce can chopped tomatoes
1 tablespoon chopped fresh oregano
1 1/2 teaspoons chopped fresh thyme
Fresh oregano or thyme sprigs, to
   garnish
Freshly cooked spaghetti, to serve

1 Put the flour in a plastic bag and season with salt and pepper; shake to mix. Drop the chicken pieces into the bag, one at a time, and shake to coat with the flour. Gently tap off any excess and put the floured chicken on a plate.

2 Heat the oil in a casserole over medium-high heat. Add the chicken and cook until golden on all sides, turning as necessary. Transfer to a plate.

3 Add the onion and mushrooms to the oil still in the casserole, adding a little more if needed, and cook, stirring frequently, for 7 minutes, or until golden. Add the garlic and cook for a further 20–30 seconds.

4 Pour in the wine and stir to scrape up any cooking residue on the casserole, then add the broth or water and the tomatoes. Season with salt and pepper and replace the chicken with any juices that have seeped from it.

5 Bring to a boil, reduce the heat to low, and cover the casserole. Simmer for about 40 minutes, or until the chicken is tender and cooked through and the juices are thickened. Baste the chicken occasionally, if necessary, during cooking.

6 Tilt the casserole to skim off any excess fat, then stir in the chopped herbs. Garnish with oregano or thyme sprigs and serve with freshly cooked spaghetti.

Menu

Chicken Hunter-style
~
Luxury
Mashed Potatoes
(p.166)
~
Hot Vegetable Salad
(p.184)
~
Pumpkin Pie (p.220)

Chicken & Sausage Gumbo

Serves 4

3 tablespoons light olive oil

12 ounces smoked sausage such as *kielbasa*, cut into 2-inch slices

2 pounds chicken thighs, cut in half

1 onion, finely chopped

2 ribs celery, finely sliced

2 cloves garlic, crushed

1 green bell pepper, seeded and finely chopped

2 tablespoons flour

14-ounce can chopped tomatoes

2 cups chicken broth

Salt and freshly ground black pepper

2 tablespoons chopped fresh parsley

Menu

Chicken & Sausage Gumbo

~

Old-fashioned Cornbread (p.210)

~

Poached Pears with Maple Syrup & Pecans (p.218)

1 Heat 2 tablespoons oil in a large casserole. Add the sausage slices and brown for 3–4 minutes. Remove with a slotted spoon and set aside.

2 Add the chicken pieces and brown, a few at a time, for 3–4 minutes. Remove with a slotted spoon and combine with the sausage.

3 Pour the remaining oil into the casserole. Add the onion, celery, garlic, and pepper and cook, stirring to prevent them burning, for 10 minutes. Stir in the flour and cook for a further 5 minutes.

4 Add the tomatoes and chicken broth, then bring to a boil. Add the sausage and chicken, stir well, and season with salt and pepper. Cover and simmer gently for 40 minutes. Check the seasoning and just before serving stir in the parsley.

Honey-orange Chicken

Serves 4

One 3-pound chicken
Juice of 2 oranges (about ¾ cup)
3 cloves garlic, crushed
5 tablespoons honey
1 tablespoon chopped chipotles in
  adobo

1 Stand the chicken on a cutting board with its tail end upwards. Using a large, sharp knife or poultry shears, cut down one side of the backbone. Repeat down the other side of the backbone and remove it.

2 Lay the chicken, skin side up, and press down to crack the breastbone and flatten the bird.

3 In a non-metallic dish large enough to hold the bird, mix together the orange juice, garlic, honey, and chipotles. Add the chicken, skin side down, and marinate in the refrigerator for about 1 hour.

4 Preheat a gas grill to medium direct heat.

5 Wrap 2 average-sized bricks in a double thickness of aluminum foil. Put the chicken, skin side down, on the grill and top with a baking sheet. Put the bricks on top of the baking sheet.

6 Grill for 5 minutes, then remove the baking sheet and bricks and turn the chicken over. Brush with any remaining marinade. Replace the baking sheet and bricks. Keep removing the bricks and turning every 5–10 minutes, brushing with the marinade, for a total cooking time of about 35 minutes, ending skin side down. The chicken should be golden and the skin very crisp. The juices should run clear.

7 Transfer the chicken to a clean cutting board and cut in half through the breastbone. Remove the leg quarters and separate the drumsticks from the thighs. Cut the breasts in half crossways to give 8 pieces. Serve immediately.

Menu

*Honey-orange
Chicken*

~

*Luxury Mashed
Potato (p.166)*

~

*Braised Fennel
(p.177)*

Chicken Kiev

Serves 4

1 stick (8 tablespoons) butter, softened
1 tablespoon lemon juice
1 clove garlic, mashed with a little salt
1 tablespoon finely chopped fresh
  parsley
4 large part-boned chicken breasts,
  with wings attached, skinned
Salt and freshly ground black pepper
$\frac{1}{2}$ cup all-purpose flour
2 eggs
1 cup fresh white bread crumbs
Vegetable oil, for deep-frying
Fresh parsley sprigs, to garnish

1 Cream the butter, lemon juice, garlic, and parsley in a small bowl until well blended. Chill until beginning to firm up, about 20 minutes.

2 Place each chicken breast between plastic wrap and gently roll the meat with a rolling pin to flatten it without making any holes in it. Turn the breasts with the wings down and season.

3 Scrape the butter onto a piece of plastic wrap and roll into a thin sausage shape. Cut into 4 pieces and lay a piece on each chicken breast.

4 Starting at the far end, roll up the chicken fillet around the butter towards the wing joint, tucking in the sides. Make sure the butter is completely enclosed.

5 Put the flour in a plastic bag and put a chicken breast in the bag. Twist the bag to close the end and roll the chicken gently to coat it completely in flour. Repeat with the remaining chicken.

6 Beat the eggs in a shallow bowl and put the bread crumbs in another bowl. Dip a piece of floured chicken in the egg, turning to coat the entire portion, then into the bread crumbs, rolling to coat it completely. Repeat with the remaining chicken, egg, and bread crumbs. Arrange on a plate, cover, and chill for at least 2 hours or overnight.

7 Heat the oil for deep-frying to 365°F, or until a small cube of day-old bread browns in about 60 seconds. Add the chicken pieces and deep-fry gently for about 5 minutes, turning once, until crisp and golden. Drain well on paper towels and serve immediately, garnished with parsley.

Menu

Chicken Kiev
~
Duchesse Potatoes
(p.166)
~
Spiced Zucchini
(p.185)
~
Mango Ice Cream
(p.216)

Roast Stuffed Chicken

Serves 4

5 ounces sliced white bread, crusts
  removed
$^1/_3$ stick (3 tablespoons) butter, softened
1 onion, chopped
1 rib celery, finely chopped
1 clove garlic, crushed
4 ounces pork sausagemeat, crumbled
Zest of $^1/_2$ lemon
1 egg, lightly beaten
1 tablespoon chopped fresh sage
$^1/_2$ teaspoon paprika
Salt and freshly ground black pepper
One 3-pound chicken
Whole fresh sage leaves and thyme
  sprigs

For the gravy
2 teaspoons all-purpose flour
$^1/_2$ cup red or white wine
$1^1/_4$ cups chicken broth

1 Preheat the oven to 425°F. Cut the bread into
½-inch cubes and put them into a large bowl.
Set the bowl aside.

2 Melt 1½ tablespoons of the butter in a skillet
over a medium heat until foaming. Add the
onion and celery and cook for 5–7 minutes until softened and translucent. Add the garlic and cook for a further minute. Add the sausagemeat. Increase the heat and cook for a further 5 minutes, stirring once or twice only, until the sausagemeat is browned and cooked through. Remove any excess fat that may have come from the sausagemeat with a metal spoon and discard.

3 Add the sausagemeat mixture, lemon zest, egg,
sage, and paprika to the bread. Season well
with salt and pepper and mix together thoroughly.

4 Wash the chicken inside and out and dry with
paper towels. Turn the bird so that the wings
are nearest you with the breast uppermost. Take a handful of the stuffing mixture and put it under the flap of skin between the wings—you'll probably fit two handfuls. Press in well, then pull the skin down to cover the stuffing. Using poultry skewers or

continued on page 36

Menu

Roast Stuffed Chicken
~
*Brussels Sprouts
with Sweet Potatoes
(p.183)*
~
*Carrots with Maple
Syrup (p.182)*

toothpicks, secure the skin underneath the bird. Take the remaining stuffing and stuff the body cavity.

5 Smear the breast and legs of the chicken with the remaining butter. Season well and sprinkle with sage leaves and thyme.

6 Put the chicken into a roasting pan and cook for about 1 hour 20 minutes, or allowing 20 minutes per pound plus 20 minutes, reducing the oven temperature to 375°F after the first 20 minutes. Every 20 minutes or so, carefully baste the bird with the juices in the pan.

7 To check if the bird is cooked, remove it from the oven. Using a skewer or small sharp knife, pierce the bird in the thickest part of the thigh. If the juices run clear, without a trace of pink, the bird is cooked. Gently pull the leg away from the body. If it gives easily, the bird is cooked. Transfer the bird to a carving board and let rest for at least 10 minutes. Remove the stuffing from the body cavity and transfer to a serving dish. Sprinkle with more sage leaves and thyme sprigs, if desired. Keep warm. Carve the bird and serve with gravy.

8 To make the gravy, after transferring the bird to a carving board, remove as much fat as possible from the roasting pan. Tilt the pan so that all the juices collect in one corner and, using a large metal spoon, skim the fat off the top and discard. Put the pan over a medium heat. Add the flour and whisk well until smooth. Gradually add the red or white wine. Bring to a boil and simmer gently for 2–3 minutes until thickened. Gradually add the chicken broth, or a combination of chicken broth and the cooking water from the vegetables or potatoes. Whisk until smooth. Bring to a boil and simmer for 5–7 minutes until thickened and reduced. Taste for seasoning. Simmer for a few more minutes to reduce if the flavor is weak. Taste again and add seasoning as necessary.

Stuffing Variation

Add 1 peeled, chopped apple and 2 tablespoons of chopped walnuts to the bread along with the sausagemeat mixture. Cook 1½ cups of mixed long-grain and wild rice according to the packet instructions until tender. Add 4 chopped spring onions, 1 shredded carrot, 1½ cups sliced mushrooms, 1 crushed clove garlic, 2 tablespoons soy sauce, 1 tablespoon honey, and 1 tablespoon vegetable oil and mix well. Use to stuff the bird and cook as above.

Grilled Spiced Chicken

Serves 4

2 tablespoons fennel seeds
1 tablespoon coriander seeds
1 tablespoon black peppercorns
1½ teaspoons dried red pepper flakes
2 teaspoons cayenne pepper
2 tablespoons salt
1 teaspoon ground cinnamon
One 3-pound chicken

1 Preheat the grill to medium indirect heat. Heat a small, dry skillet on the stovetop over a medium heat and add the fennel seeds, coriander seeds, and black peppercorns. Cook for 1–2 minutes, shaking the pan frequently, until the spices smell aromatic and begin to brown. If you have an exhaust fan, switch it on full; if not, open the window and add the pepper flakes to the pan. Stand back to avoid the fumes and shake the pan for about 30 seconds. Remove the pan from the heat and quickly transfer the mixture to a plate to cool.

2 When the mixture is cool, transfer to a mortar and pestle or spice grinder and grind to a fine powder. Stir in the cayenne pepper, salt, and cinnamon.

3 Wash the chicken inside and out and dry thoroughly with paper towels. Sprinkle about 2 tablespoons of the spice mixture inside the chicken and all over the skin, rubbing it in well. If you have time, set aside to marinate for at least 30 minutes.

4 Cook the chicken over indirect medium heat for 1 hour 20 minutes, or until golden and the juices run clear. The legs should pull away from the body easily—if they don't, cook the chicken for a further 10 minutes then try again.

5 Remove the chicken from the grill and let rest for 10 minutes before carving. Otherwise, leave until cold and carve or tear the meat from the bones to use in another recipe.

Menu

Grilled Spiced Chicken

~

Latkes (p.171)

~

Cauliflower & Leek Patties (p.188)

~

Summer Berry Shortcakes (p.246)

Chicken & Vegetable Pie

Serves 4–6

One 3-pound chicken
1 large carrot, cut into chunks
1 onion, halved
1 stick celery, cut into chunks
1 bay leaf
1 fresh thyme sprig
6 black peppercorns
Salt and freshly ground black pepper
1 pound mixed spring vegetables
  (green beans, baby carrots, asparagus,
  peas, leeks, zucchini, fennel)
1/3 stick (3 tablespoons) butter
2 teaspoons fresh thyme leaves
1/3 cup all-purpose flour
1/2 cup heavy cream
1 1/4 pounds puff pastry dough
1 egg, beaten

1 Put the chicken, carrot, onion, celery, bay leaf, thyme sprig, peppercorns, and enough water to cover in a large pan, cover and gently simmer for 1 hour, skimming off any scum from the surface. Remove the pan from the heat and leave the chicken and broth to cool. Remove the chicken and set aside. Strain the broth into a clean pan and bring back to a boil. Simmer until reduced to 4 cups. Season. Skin the chicken and cut the flesh into chunks.

2 Slice the spring vegetables. Place in the boiling broth and bring back to a boil. Blanch for 3 minutes. Remove with a slotted spoon and set aside, reserving the broth. Melt the butter in a pan, add the thyme leaves and flour and stir well. Gradually add the reserved broth, stirring well, until smooth. Increase the heat, bring to a boil, stirring continuously, and simmer for 2 minutes. Remove from the heat and stir in the cream, reserved chicken, and vegetables. Season.

3 Preheat the oven to 400°F. Roll out the prepared pastry on a lightly floured surface and cut a strip just larger than the rim of the pie dish. Brush the rim of the dish with water and attach the strip. Cut another piece to make the lid. Spoon the filling into the pie dish. Dampen the pastry strip and top with the pastry lid. Cut a small slit in the center of the lid. Crimp the edges to make a decorative edge. Use pastry trimmings to decorate the pie, then brush with beaten egg. Transfer to the center of the oven and bake for 25 minutes, or until the pastry is golden and the filling is bubbling.

Menu

*Chicken &
Vegetable Pie*
~
*Spiced
Baked Apples
(p.224)*

Spicy Peanut Chicken
Noodles

Serves 4

4 ounces flat rice noodles
Salt
2 tablespoons chunky peanut butter
Pinch of ground red chile
1 tablespoon dark soy sauce
$^3/_4$ cup coconut milk
$^1/_2$ cup hot water
2 cooked chicken breast fillets,
 shredded
4 scallions sliced
Small bunch of fresh cilantro, roughly
 chopped
Green salad, to serve

Menu

Spicy
Peanut Chicken
Noodles
~
Apple Cake
Bars
(p.241)

Tip
Although this recipe calls for chicken breast fillets, if you happen to have any leftover cold roast chicken or pork in the refrigerator, these will work just as well.

1 Cook the noodles in a saucepan of boiling salted water for 4 minutes, or until tender, then drain well.

2 Meanwhile, put the peanut butter in a small saucepan with the ground red chile, soy sauce, coconut milk, and hot water.

3 Stir over a gentle heat until combined, then add the chicken and scallions. Warm through for a few minutes, and then stir in the noodles and cilantro. Serve immediately with a green salad.

Chicken Tikka

Serves 6

6 chicken breast fillets, each cut into
   8 pieces
1 yellow onion, coarsely chopped
3 cloves garlic, coarsely chopped
1 inch fresh ginger, peeled
1 cup plain yogurt
2 tablespoons toasted sesame oil
Juice of $\frac{1}{2}$ lemon
3 teaspoons ground cilantro
1 teaspoon ground turmeric
1 teaspoon dried red pepper flakes
1 teaspoon salt
1 onion, cut into quarters and
   separated into layers
Steamed spinach, to serve

1 Put the chicken in a large non-metallic bowl and set aside.

2 Put the chopped onion, garlic and ginger in a food processor and process to make a smooth paste. Add the yogurt, sesame oil, lemon juice, cilantro, turmeric, pepper flakes, and salt, and process until smooth.

Menu

Chicken Tikka
~
Coconut Rice
(p.206)

3 Pour the marinade over the chicken, toss to coat, then marinate in the refrigerator overnight. Stir to redistribute the marinade. Soak 12 bamboo skewers in water overnight.

4 Assemble the tikka kabobs. Thread four pieces of chicken on to each skewer, alternating each piece with an onion layer. Baste the kabobs with more marinade, cover, and return to the refrigerator until ready to cook.

5 To cook, prepare an outdoor grill, or preheat the broiler. Cook for several minutes on each side, turning once. Serve with steamed spinach.

Lemon Chicken
with Herb Tagliatelle

Serves 2

2 large boned chicken breasts, skin on
2 tablespoons all-purpose flour, well
  seasoned
1/3 stick (3 tablespoons) butter
1 tablespoon olive oil
Salt and freshly ground black pepper
6 1/2 ounces fresh tagliatelle
1/4 cup chopped fresh herbs
2 teaspoons grated lemon zest
2 tablespoons fresh lemon juice
1 tablespoon drained capers, roughly
  chopped if large

1 Wash and dry the chicken breasts. Put the seasoned flour on to a plate and coat both sides of each chicken breast. Shake to remove any excess flour. Set aside.

2 Melt half the butter with the oil in a skillet until foaming. Add the chicken breasts, skin side down, and cook for about 10 minutes over low heat until deep golden.

Menu

Lemon
Chicken with Herb
Tagliatelle
~
Zucchini Bread
(p.208)
~
Peanut Butter
Brownies
(p.240)

3 Turn the chicken breasts and cook on the second side for a further 10 minutes.

4 Turn the chicken breasts again and cook for a further 5–10 minutes, or until the chicken is cooked through.

5 Meanwhile, bring a large saucepan of salted water to a boil. Add the pasta and cook for 2–3 minutes, or until al dente. Drain well, then sprinkle in the chopped fresh herbs and stir.

6 Remove the cooked chicken breasts from the pan. Add the remaining butter and cook until foaming and beginning to brown. Add the lemon zest and juice and the capers. Scrape up any bits from the bottom of the pan. Remove from the heat and season.

7 Slice the chicken breasts thickly on the diagonal. Divide the pasta among serving dishes and top with the sliced chicken. Drizzle with the lemon butter sauce and serve immediately.

Spicy Chicken Sausages

Serves 4

1½ tablespoons butter
1 onion, finely chopped
2 cloves garlic, finely chopped
1 tablespoon paprika
1¼ pounds boned chicken thighs
2 fresh red hot chiles, seeded
Small bunch of fresh parsley
10 thyme sprigs
½ cup fresh white bread crumbs
1 egg, beaten
Salt and freshly ground black pepper
4 tablespoons sunflower oil

1 Melt the butter in a skillet. Add the onion and garlic and fry for 5 minutes. Add the paprika and fry for 1 minute. Take off the heat and let cool.

2 Put the boneless chicken thighs in a food processor and process for a few seconds until the meat is finely chopped. Don't over-process or it will become a paste. Transfer to a mixing bowl.

3 Finely chop the chiles, parsley, and thyme with a mezzaluna, and mix into the chopped chicken with the cooled onion mixture and bread crumbs. Add the beaten egg and stir well. Season well with salt and pepper.

4 Divide the mixture into 12 balls and roll the sausages. Heat the oil in a skillet and fry the sausages, turning regularly, for 15–20 minutes, or until browned and cooked through.

Menu

Spicy Chicken Sausages

~

Beet & Onion Mash
(p.182)

~

New England
Blueberry Pancakes
(p.226)

Apple & Ginger Turkey Sandwiches

Serves 4

4 turkey breast steaks
1 large onion, thickly sliced
1 tablespoon olive oil
2 dessert apples, such as Granny Smith,
  cored and thickly sliced crossways
Ciabatta bread
Salt and freshly ground black pepper
Mayonnaise
Arugula leaves, to serve

For the apple marinade
$1/2$ cup apple cider, preferably fresh
2 tablespoons cider vinegar
2 teaspoons finely grated fresh ginger
1 clove garlic, crushed
3 cloves

1 For the marinade, mix the apple cider, cider vinegar, ginger, garlic, and cloves together in a small saucepan over a low heat. Bring to a boil and simmer for 2 minutes, then remove from the heat. Let cool.

Menu

Apple & Ginger Turkey Sandwiches
~
Classic Coleslaw (p.191)

2 Put the turkey steaks in a single layer in a non-metallic dish. Pour the cooled marinade over, then marinate in the refrigerator for at least 1 hour.

3 Preheat the grill to high direct heat. Brush the onion slices with the olive oil and cook over high direct heat for 10-12 minutes, turning often and carefully, until golden and tender.

4 Cook the apple slices with the onions for 4-5 minutes, turning often until golden and tender.

5 Lift the turkey steaks from the marinade, shaking off the excess. Cook, alongside the onion and apple slices, over high direct heat for 6-8 minutes, turning once halfway through the cooking time.

6 Top the ciabatta bread with a turkey steak, some onion, 2 apple slices, and some mayonnaise. Serve with a few arugula leaves.

Roast Turkey with

Sausage & Sage Stuffing

Serves 10–12

One 10–12 pound turkey with giblets,
  neck and wing tips removed for gravy
2 sticks (16 tablespoons) butter, softened
$\frac{1}{2}$ teaspoon dried thyme
$\frac{1}{2}$ teaspoon dried sage
2 cups chicken or turkey broth
Watercress or herb sprigs, to garnish

For the stuffing
1½ tablespoons butter
1 onion, chopped
2–3 ribs celery, thinly sliced
16 ounces sausagemeat
2 cloves garlic, crushed
2 tablespoons chopped sage
1 tablespoon dried thyme
1 cup pecans, toasted and chopped
  (optional)
1 pound firm-textured white bread,
  crusts removed, cut into small cubes
2–3 cups chicken or turkey broth,
  preferably homemade
Salt and freshly ground black pepper
2 eggs, lightly beaten

1 To prepare the stuffing, melt the butter in a large saucepan. Add the onion and celery and cook, stirring frequently, for about 4 minutes, until the vegetables begin to soften. Add the sausagemeat and garlic and cook, stirring, for 4 minutes, until the meat is no longer pink. Stir in the sage, thyme, and pecans, if using, and remove from the heat.

2 Add the bread to the stuffing and combine it with the other ingredients. Stir in half the broth and season with salt and pepper. Add more broth if the mixture seems dry, then let cool slightly.

3 Stir the beaten eggs into the stuffing. Add more broth, if necessary, so that the stuffing holds together but is not too wet. Set aside. (This can be prepared a day ahead, covered, and chilled.)

4 To prepare the turkey, preheat the oven to 325°F. Rinse the turkey cavity and dry with

Menu

*Roast Turkey
with Sausage & Sage
Stuffing*

~

*Sweet Potato Casserole
with Marshmallow
Topping (p.176)*

~

*Braised Sugar Snaps
with Lettuce (p.178)*

~

*Double-crust Apple Pie
(p.228)*

paper towels, then season. Cream the butter, thyme, sage, and salt and pepper together in a bowl. Starting with the neck end, separate the skin from the meat on both sides of the breast. Spread half the butter under the skin, pushing it far under the skin. Rub the remaining butter over the turkey. Tuck the neck skin under the bird and close with a skewer.

5 Spoon the stuffing into the cavity and secure the opening with skewers. Tie the legs together with string. Alternatively, stuff the neck end before tucking the skin under and securing it. Put any leftover stuffing in a greased baking dish and cover with foil—this can be baked in the oven with the turkey for about 1 hour at the end of cooking.

6 Set the turkey on a rack in a roasting pan and pour about 1 cup of the broth into the pan. Roast the turkey for 3½-4½ hours, or until a meat

thermometer inserted into the thickest part of the thigh reads 180°F. Baste the turkey frequently, adding a little more broth or water as necessary. Check the cooking after 3 hours by piercing a thigh with a skewer—the juices should run clear, if not, continue cooking. Cover the turkey with foil if it browns too quickly. Transfer it to a plate and leave, covered with a tent of foil, for at least 30 minutes.

7 To serve, remove the skewers and spoon the stuffing into a serving bowl; keep warm. Carve the turkey on to a large heated platter or directly on to serving plates and serve with stuffing, gravy, and all the trimmings, and garnished with watercress sprigs.

Tip
Frozen turkeys are best thawed in the refrigerator. The key to this method is to plan ahead and allow 24 hours for every 4-5 pounds of turkey weight.

Spicy Turkey Meatballs

Serves 4

1 pound boneless turkey breast
8 ounces pancetta or bacon, chopped
2 cloves garlic, chopped
1 teaspoon salt
Pinch of ground cinnamon
Pinch of ground allspice
Large pinch of dried red pepper flakes
Salt and freshly ground black pepper
1/4 cup fresh bread crumbs
1 egg, lightly beaten
4 tablespoons olive oil
1 onion, finely chopped
2 pounds ripe tomatoes, skinned and
    roughly chopped
2/3 cup red wine
1 teaspoon dried oregano
2 tablespoons chopped fresh basil,
    plus extra to garnish
Pinch of sugar
12 ounces fresh taglioni or tagliatelle
Freshly grated Parmesan cheese,
    to serve

1 Cut the turkey into chunks and put into a food processor. Add the pancetta or bacon, garlic, salt, cinnamon, allspice, pepper flakes, and pepper. Process until finely chopped. Transfer to a bowl, add the bread crumbs and egg and mix. Shape the mixture into balls. Chill at least 30 minutes.

2 Heat 2 tablespoons of the oil, add the onion, and fry for 5 minutes. Add tomatoes, red wine, oregano, half the basil, and the sugar and bring to a boil. Cover and simmer for 30 minutes.

3 Heat the remaining oil in a skillet over medium heat. Add the meatballs in batches and cook for 5 minutes, turning frequently, until golden. As they brown, add them to the tomato sauce. Bring the sauce back to a boil and simmer for 20–30 minutes until the meatballs are cooked and the sauce is thickened. Stir in the remaining basil.

4 Meanwhile, bring a large saucepan of salted water to a rolling boil. Add the pasta and cook for 2–3 minutes until al dente. Drain well.

5 Divide the pasta among serving dishes and top with the meatball sauce. Garnish with extra basil and serve with Parmesan cheese.

Menu

Spicy Turkey Meatballs
~
Panzanella (p.198)
~
Chocolate-covered Doughnuts (p.238)

Turkey-stuffed Peppers

Serves 4

Grated zest and juice of 1 lime
4 scallions, chopped
2 cloves garlic, crushed
1 carrot, coarsely grated
8 closed-cap mushrooms, thinly sliced
Salt and freshly ground black pepper
2 tablespoons extra virgin olive oil,
    plus extra for oiling and brushing
1 pound boneless turkey breast fillets,
    cut into fine strips
4 large green bell peppers, halved and
    seeded with stalks in place
$^1/_4$ cup chopped fresh cilantro

Tip

You can vary the ingredients used to stuff these peppers. Try using chicken, pork, or lean steak. For a vegetarian version just add rice to fill it out.

1 Mix the lime zest and juice in a bowl. Add the scallions, garlic, carrot, mushrooms, and plenty of seasoning. Stir in the oil, then mix in the turkey. Cover and chill for at least 1 hour. If you can, make this in advance and chill for several hours.

2 Preheat the oven to 400°F. Oil a large, shallow ovenproof dish, then place the pepper halves in it, supporting them against each other so they sit neatly. Brush with a little oil and bake for 20 minutes.

3 Stir the turkey mixture well, then divide it among the pepper 'boats'. Drizzle with a little extra oil to moisten the filling. Bake for a further 20–30 minutes, or until both peppers and filling are well cooked and browned on top.

4 Sprinkle the chopped cilantro over the peppers and filling, and serve at once.

Menu

Turkey-stuffed Peppers
~
Chickpea & Tomato Salad
(p.195)
~
Cherry Clafoutis
(p.243)

MEAT

- Tortilla Wraps with Honey Roast Ham & Pepper Slaw
- Grilled Cheese & Tomato Sandwiches with Bacon
- Italian Submarine Sandwiches
- New Potato & Crispy Bacon Salad
- Tomato Pasta with Italian Sausage & Lentils
- Quick Mushroom Carbonara
- Chop Suey
- Cowboy Beans & Sausages
- Rice Vermicelli with Pork & Vegetables
- Spanish Pork with Tomatoes & Chorizo
- Baked Ham
- Kansas City Spareribs
- Bacon Cheeseburgers
- Beef & Onion Pies
- Pasta Shells Filled with Bolognese
- Beef Stew with Herb Dumplings
- Easy Burritos
- Rib Roast with Caramelized Shallots
- Old-fashioned Meatloaf
- Beef Stew with Star Anise
- Braised Lamb Shanks with Mirepoix Vegetables
- Tagine with Prunes & Almonds
- Lamb Meatballs with Buttermilk & Herb Dip
- Papaya Lamb Kabobs
- Kofta
- Roast Leg of Lamb
- Baked Lasagne

CHAPTER TWO

MEAT

Tortilla Wraps with

Honey Roast Ham & Pepper Slaw

Serves 4

8 soft flour tortillas
8 large thin slices honey roast ham
Few salad leaves

For the pepper slaw
1 pound white cabbage, finely
  shredded
8 ounces carrots, grated
2 red bell peppers, seeded and thinly
  sliced
1 cup mayonnaise
$^3/_4$ cup sour cream or plain yogurt
1 teaspoon white wine vinegar
Salt and freshly ground black pepper

Menu

*Tortilla Wraps with
Honey Roast Ham &
Pepper Slaw*

~

*Warm Cheese &
Chipotle Dip with
Tortilla Chips (p.163)*

~

*Summer Berry
Shortcakes (p.246)*

1 For the pepper slaw, mix the cabbage, carrots, and peppers together in a large bowl. Mix the mayonnaise with the sour cream and vinegar, and season with salt and pepper.

2 Take 8 tortillas and place a slice of ham in the top center of each one. Spoon 2-3 tablespoons of the slaw on top with a few salad leaves. Bring up the bottom of the wrap and fold in the sides.

3 Secure each wrap with a toothpick and wrap in a napkin.

Grilled Cheese & Tomato
Sandwiches with Bacon

Serves 4

8 slices country-style white bread
½ stick (4 tablespoons) butter, softened
2 tablespoons Dijon mustard
4–6 ounces Swiss cheese, such as
   Emmental, thinly sliced
4–6 ounces cheddar cheese,
   thinly sliced
8 thick tomato slices
8 slices lean bacon, cooked until crisp
Potato chips, to serve

Menu

Grilled Cheese &
Tomato Sandwiches
with Bacon
~
Caesar Salad (p.194)
~
Apple Sauce Sundae
(p.236)

1 Lay the slices of bread on a board and spread them evenly with butter. Turn the slices over, so the buttered sides are down, and spread the other sides with the mustard.

2 Layer the cheeses, tomato slices and bacon on 4 bread slices, overlapping or trimming the ingredients to fit. Top with the remaining bread, mustard sides down, and press gently to compress the sandwiches.

3 Heat a large, non-stick skillet over medium heat.

4 Working in batches, place the sandwiches in the pan and cook for about 3 minutes, pressing down gently and frequently until crisp and golden. Carefully turn and continue cooking for a further 2 minutes, pressing the sandwiches down until they are golden and the cheese is melting and beginning to ooze out. Repeat with the remaining sandwiches.

5 Transfer the sandwiches to a cutting board and slice in half. Serve immediately with some potato chips.

Italian Submarine

Sandwiches

Serves 4

¹/₂ cup mayonnaise

¹/₄ cup sour cream

1 tablespoon Dijon mustard

4 individual French rolls, about
   8 inches long

Butter or margarine, softened, for
   spreading

Crisp lettuce leaves

6 ounces boiled or baked ham, sliced

6 ounces salami

6 ounces cooked chicken or turkey,
   sliced

3 ounces Emmental cheese, sliced

3 ounces cheddar cheese, sliced

2 tomatoes, thinly sliced

1 large green bell pepper, seeded and
   cut into rings

1 onion, thinly sliced

Menu

*Italian
Submarine
Sandwiches*
~
*Chef's Salad
(p.197)*

1 Combine the mayonnaise, sour cream, and mustard in a small bowl until well blended.

2 Using a serrated knife, split the rolls horizontally in half. Remove some of the soft bread and spread both halves lightly with butter or margarine. Spread the top halves generously with the mayonnaise mixture.

3 Arrange 2-3 lettuce leaves on the bottom half of each roll, folding them to fit. Layer the remaining ingredients in order on top of the lettuce. Cover with the tops and cut across in half.

New Potato & Crispy Bacon Salad

Serves 4

2¼ pounds small new potatoes, scrubbed

Salt and freshly ground black pepper

10 ounces asparagus spears, woody stalks removed

6 cloves garlic, unpeeled

6 tablespoons vegetable oil

6 ounces streaky bacon rashers

7 ounces blue cheese, crumbled

2 tablespoons chopped fresh parsley

1 tablespoon snipped fresh chives

1 Preheat the oven to 400°F. Put the new potatoes in a saucepan of salted water. Bring to a boil and cook for 5 minutes. Drain and put in a roasting pan with the asparagus and garlic. Season with salt and pepper and drizzle with oil. Roast in the oven for 45 minutes.

2 Meanwhile, lay the bacon in another roasting pan and cook in the oven for 10-15 minutes until brown and crispy. Remove and let cool. Crumble the bacon into small pieces.

3 Once the potatoes are cooked, discard the garlic. Put the potatoes in a serving dish with the asparagus, set aside until just warm, then scatter with the bacon, blue cheese, and herbs. Serve warm or cold.

Menu

New Potato & Crispy Bacon Salad

~

Emmental & Roasted Corn Spoon Bread (p.207)

~

Boston Cream Pie (p.244)

Tomato Pasta with
Italian Sausage & Lentils

Serves 4

1½ cups green French lentils
3 tablespoons olive oil
1 onion, finely chopped
1 pound spicy Italian sausage
2 cloves garlic, crushed
14-ounce can chopped tomatoes
1¼ cups chicken or vegetable broth
Salt and freshly ground black pepper
12 ounces fresh tomato-flavored
    tagliatelle
1 tablespoon chopped fresh parsley

1 Pick over the lentils, looking for any grit. Rinse under cold running water and drain well.

2 Heat the oil in a large, deep saucepan and add the onion. Cook for 5-7 minutes over a low heat until soft and starting to brown. Add the sausages and garlic and cook for 3-4 minutes until the sausages start to brown. Add the drained lentils and continue cooking for a further 1 minute.

3 Add the tomatoes and broth. Season lightly with salt and pepper and bring to a boil. Cover, reduce the heat and simmer gently for 40-45 minutes until the sausages and lentils are tender. Check the seasoning.

4 Meanwhile, bring a large saucepan of salted water to a rolling boil. Add the pasta and cook for 2-3 minutes until al dente. Drain well.

5 Divide the pasta among serving dishes and spoon over the sausages and lentils. Sprinkle with the chopped parsley and serve.

Menu

*Tomato Pasta
with Italian Sausage
& Lentils*
~
*Green Bean &
Mozzarella Salad
(p.201)*
~
*Spiced Baked Apples
(p.224)*

Quick Mushroom
Carbonara

Serves 4

12 ounces dried spaghetti
Salt and freshly ground black pepper
²/₃ cup heavy cream
1 clove garlic
5 ounces pancetta or country ham
  cubes
8 cremini mushrooms, sliced
4 egg yolks, beaten
3 tablespoons freshly grated
  Parmesan cheese

Menu

*Quick Mushroom
Carbonara*

~

*Hot Vegetable Salad
(p.184)*

~

*Chocolate Fondue
with Marshmallows
(p.230)*

1 Cook the spaghetti in a saucepan of salted boiling water according to the instructions on the packet until al dente. Drain well. Meanwhile, put the cream and garlic clove in a saucepan and bring to a boil. Set aside.

2 Heat a skillet. Add the pancetta or country ham and mushrooms and fry for 4–5 minutes, or until browned. Toss with the spaghetti.

3 Remove the garlic from the cream and pour over the spaghetti. Quickly stir in the egg yolks and Parmesan cheese. Season to taste with salt and pepper and serve immediately.

Chop Suey

Serves 4

Menu

Chop Suey

~

*Tropical
Fruit Salad
(p.221)*

2 tablespoons cornstarch

3 tablespoons soy sauce

1 tablespoon dry sherry

Salt and freshly ground black pepper

1-inch piece fresh ginger, grated or
 finely chopped

$\frac{1}{2}$ cup water

2 tablespoons vegetable oil

1 pound pork tenderloin or skinless,
 boneless chicken breast, cut into thin
 strips

1 small head Chinese cabbage, finely
 shredded

2–3 ribs celery, thinly sliced on the
 diagonal into $\frac{1}{2}$-inch pieces

6–8 scallions, sliced on the diagonal
 into $\frac{1}{2}$-inch pieces

1 pound bean sprouts, rinsed

6–8 ounce can water chestnuts, drained
 and sliced

5–6 ounce can bamboo shoots, drained
 and sliced

2 tablespoons chopped fresh cilantro
 leaves or parsley

Cooked rice, to serve

1 Combine the cornstarch, soy sauce, sherry, salt and pepper, ginger, and water in a small bowl until well blended; set aside.

2 Heat the oil over medium-high heat in a wok or large heavy-based skillet. Add the pork or chicken and stir-fry for about 4 minutes. Stir the cornstarch mixture and stir it into the pork—the mixture will thicken as it comes to a boil.

3 Add the cabbage, celery, scallions, bean sprouts, water chestnuts, bamboo shoots, and cilantro to the wok and stir-fry for a further 5 minutes, or until the meat is cooked and vegetables are just tender. Serve on a bed of rice.

Cowboy Beans

& Sausages

Serves 4

Menu

*Cowboy Beans &
Sausages*

~

*Maple-baked Acorn
Squash (p.189)*

~

*Applesauce Sundae
(p.236)*

1 pound dried white kidney beans
3 tablespoons oil
2 onions, roughly chopped
2 cloves garlic, crushed
14-ounce can chopped tomatoes
9 ounces smoked bacon, roughly
   chopped
1 tablespoon dark molasses
1 tablespoon mustard powder
2 tablespoons soft brown sugar
16 small sausages
Salt and freshly ground black pepper

1 Soak the beans overnight in plenty of cold water. Drain and put in a large saucepan. Cover with water, bring to a boil and boil for 15 minutes. Reduce the heat and simmer for 1 hour.

2 Meanwhile, heat the oil in a large casserole. Add the onions and garlic and cook for 15 minutes. Add the tomatoes, bacon, mollases, mustard powder, and sugar and stir well. Preheat the oven to 300°F.

3 Add the beans, cover and cook in the oven for 2 hours. Uncover and cook for a further 1 hour.

4 Preheat the broiler. Broil the sausages for 15 minutes, turning to ensure even cooking, then cut into bite-sized pieces. Stir the bacon into the beans and cook for a further 20 minutes. Taste and season with salt and pepper before serving.

Rice Vermicelli
with Pork & Vegetables

Serves 4

12 ounces rice vermicelli

16 ounces mixed vegetables (such as broccoli, snow peas and asparagus)

1 tablespoon arrowroot or cornstarch

1 teaspoon honey

$\frac{1}{2}$ cup chicken or vegetable broth

4 tablespoons vegetable oil

4 tablespoons light soy sauce

2 cloves garlic, finely chopped

1-inch piece fresh ginger, peeled and finely chopped

8 ounces lean pork, sliced into thin 1-inch squares

1 tablespoon nuoc mam (Vietnamese fish sauce)

1 tablespoon black bean sauce

1 tablespoon chopped fresh basil leaves or cilantro, to garnish

1 Cook the noodles according to the instructions on the packet. Rinse under cold running water and set aside.

2 Prepare the vegetables: cut the broccoli into florets; cut the snow peas in half; cut the asparagus into 2-inch pieces. Steam the broccoli and asparagus for 5 minutes until tender but still crisp. Refresh under cold running water and set aside.

3 Blend the arrowroot or cornstarch and honey with the broth. Set aside. Heat half the oil in a wok and add the noodles and 1 tablespoon of the soy sauce. Stir-fry for 30 seconds, then transfer to a serving platter.

4 Add the remaining oil to the wok. Stir-fry the garlic and ginger until they start to change color. Add the pork and snow peas, and stir-fry until the pork starts to brown. Add the remaining 3 tablespoons soy sauce, the nuoc mam, black bean sauce, vegetables, and broth mixture. Stir until the sauce thickens, then pour over the noodles and garnish with basil or cilantro.

Menu

Rice Vermicelli with
Pork & Vegetables
~
Chicken Satay
Skewers with Sweet
Chile Sauce
(p.22)
~
Chilled Tangerine
& Lemon Mousse
(p.233)

Spanish Pork
with Tomatoes & Chorizo

Serves 6

One 3-pound pork shoulder roast
2 tablespoons sunflower oil
2 onions, finely chopped
4 cloves garlic, finely chopped
6½ ounces chorizo sausage, skin
   removed and roughly chopped
1 tablespoon paprika
Two 14-ounce cans chopped tomatoes
½ cup white wine
2 bay leaves
Small bunch of fresh parsley, finely
   chopped
Green salad, to serve

Tip
If you cannot get hold of
pork shoulder roast, you can
get away with cheaper cuts of
pork for this recipe as it is
cooked slowly for such a
long length of time.

Menu
Spanish Pork
with Tomatoes &
Chorizo
~
Patatas Bravas
(p.167)

1 Preheat the oven to 300°F. Cut the pork into ½-inch pieces with a large chopping knife.

2 Heat the oil in a large casserole and brown the meat in batches. Transfer to a bowl. Add the onions and garlic to the casserole and fry for about 10 minutes, or until browned. Add the chorizo to the casserole and fry 5 minutes. Stir in the paprika.

3 Return the meat to the casserole and add the tomatoes, wine, and bay leaves. Cover and cook in the oven for 3 hours.

4 Sprinkle over the parsley before serving, and serve with a green salad.

Baked Ham

Serves 20–25

10½–13 pound partially cooked whole
  ham, preferably boneless
Whole cloves, for studding
Fresh parsley sprigs, to garnish
Boiled or mashed potato or salad, to serve

For the honey-mustard glaze
2 tablespoons soy sauce
¼ cup water, plus 2–3 tablespoons
1 cup honey
1 cup Dijon mustard
½–1 teaspoon cornstarch

1 Preheat the oven to 325°F. Put the ham on a rack in a large roasting pan and add enough water to cover the bottom of the pan. Insert a meat thermometer in the thickest part of the ham and roast, uncovered, allowing 20–25 minutes per pound or until the thermometer reaches 160°F. Add more water if needed during cooking to prevent the ham from drying out.

2 About 1 hour before the ham is ready, combine the soy sauce, ¼ cup water, honey, and mustard for the glaze in a small pan. Bring to a boil over a medium heat, stirring, and then remove from the heat.

3 Remove the ham from the oven and cut off any rind, leaving a thick layer of white fat. Slash the surface of the fat diagonally to create a diamond pattern and press a clove in the middle of each diamond. Brush with the glaze and roast for a further 45 minutes, brushing with more glaze occasionally. Keep the bottom of the roasting pan covered with water. Transfer the ham to a serving platter and tent it with foil but do not let the foil stick to the glazed surface. Set aside.

4 Tilt the roasting pan and skim off any fat from the pan, then add the remaining glaze to the pan and set it over a medium heat. Stir 2–3 tablespoons water into the cornstarch until smooth, then stir it into the glaze and bring to a boil, stirring, until lightly thickened. Add more blended cornstarch or water, as necessary, and add any juices from the baked ham. Strain into a gravy boat.

5 Garnish the ham with parsley and serve hot with the glaze as a sauce.

Menu

Baked Ham
~
*Luxury Mashed
Potatoes (p.166)*
~
*Braised Fennel
(p.177)*
~
*Cherry Clafoutis
(p.243)*

Kansas City Spareribs

Serves 4

$^1/_3$ cup dark brown sugar
$^1/_2$ onion, finely chopped
$1^1/_2$ teaspoons celery seeds
$1^1/_2$ teaspoons garlic powder
$1^1/_2$ teaspoons chili powder
1 teaspoon finely ground black pepper
1 teaspoon ground cumin
$^1/_2$ teaspoon cayenne pepper
2 cups tomato ketchup
$^1/_4$ cup white vinegar or more to taste
2 tablespoons prepared yellow
  mustard
Juice of 1 lime
1 teaspoon liquid smoke (optional)
Salt and freshly ground black pepper
$^1/_2$ stick (4 tablespoons) butter, cubed
6 pounds baby back pork spareribs

Menu

*Kansas City
Pork Ribs*

~

*Spiced Grilled
Sweet Potatoes
(p.170)*

~

*Chickpea &
Tomato Salad
(p.195)*

1 Preheat a gas grill to medium indirect heat. Combine all the ingredients, except the butter and spareribs in a medium saucepan. Bring to a boil, stirring to dissolve the sugar. You may want to have a lid handy to protect yourself and your kitchen from any sputtering. Reduce the heat and simmer for 25 minutes, stirring occasionally. With a whisk, blend in the butter cubes, a couple at a time, until incorporated. Set aside until needed.

2 Cook the ribs on the grill for $1-1^1/_4$ hours, turning once halfway through cooking time, until very tender. Brush generously with the sauce during the last 10 minutes of cooking time.

3 Remove from the grill and let rest for 10 minutes. Carve into individual ribs and serve immediately with extra sauce.

Bacon Cheeseburgers

Serves 4

1¾ pounds minced beef (not too lean)
Salt and freshly ground black pepper
4–6 slices bacon, cut in half
4 slices cheddar cheese
4 sesame buns, split and toasted
Lettuce leaves
Sliced onion, mayonnaise, tomato
  ketchup, and pickles, to taste

Menu

Bacon
Cheeseburgers
~
Tomato Salsa (p.162)
~
Old-fashioned
English Chips (p.164)
~
Berry Frozen Treats
(p.214)

1 Gently break the beef apart in a bowl with a fork. Season with salt and pepper, and shape into 4 large patties. Chill until ready to cook.

2 Put the bacon rashers in a heavy-based skillet and cook over a medium heat for about 6 minutes, or until crisp and browned, turning once. Drain on paper towels.

3 Pour off all but 2 tablespoons of the bacon fat and add the burgers to the pan. Cook until browned and juicy, turning once. Allow 6 minutes for rare or 7–8 minutes for a well-done burger. Just before the burgers are ready, top each with a slice of cheese and cook until the cheese begins to soften.

4 Arrange a lettuce leaf on the bottom of each bun, then place a burger on top. Add the bacon and a selection of condiments. Cover with the bun top and serve immediately.

Beef & Onion Pies

Serves 4

4 tablespoons vegetable oil

2 large onions, sliced

1 teaspoon brown sugar

1½ pounds lean rump steak, cubed

2 tablespoons all-purpose flour

1 carrot, finely chopped

2 cloves garlic, finely chopped

8 ounces baby button or baby cremini mushrooms

⅔ cup beef broth

⅔ cup stout or other dark beer

1 tablespoon tomato paste

1 tablespoon Worcestershire sauce

1 tablespoon fresh thyme leaves

1 bay leaf

12 ounces potatoes, peeled and cubed

10 ounces frozen puff pastry, thawed

1 egg, beaten

Menu

Beef & Onion Pies
~
Roasted Vegetables with Pine Nuts & Parmesan (p.187)
~
Sticky Toffee Pudding (p.225)

1 Heat half the oil in a large skillet. Add the onions and cook for 5–7 minutes over medium heat until lightly golden. Stir in the sugar and cook for 4–5 minutes until caramelized. Set aside.

2 Preheat the oven to 275°F. Toss the meat in the flour, shaking off and reserving any excess. Heat the remaining oil over medium heat in a large casserole and add the meat. Cook for 5–7 minutes until brown. Add the carrot, garlic, and mushrooms and cook for 3–4 minutes until softened. Stir in the rest of the flour. Gradually add the broth and stout.

3 Add the tomato paste, Worcestershire sauce, thyme, and bay leaf. Bring to a boil, cover, and cook in the oven for 1 hour. Add the potatoes and cook for 20 minutes until tender. Increase the oven temperature to 400°F. Spoon the steak mixture into 4 individual ovenproof pie dishes. Top with the onions.

4 Roll the pastry out thinly and cut 4 ovals or rounds about 2 inches wider than the pie dishes. From these, trim a 1-inch wide strip. Wet the rims of the dishes and attach the pastry strips. Wet the pastry strips and attach the pastry lids. Seal and make a decorative edge. Decorate with trimmings.

5 Brush the pastry with beaten egg. Bake for 25 minutes until the pastry is risen and golden. Let cool slightly before serving.

Pasta Shells
Filled with Bolognese Sauce

Menu

*Pasta Shells
Filled with Bolognese*
~
Panzanella (p.198)
~
*Poached Pears
with Maple Syrup
& Pecans
(p.218)*

Serves 4

3 tablespoons vegetable oil
1 onion, finely chopped
1 clove garlic, crushed
2 ribs celery, finely chopped
3 slices streaky bacon
1½ pounds ground beef
14½-ounce can chopped tomatoes
3 tablespoons tomato purée
1 teaspoon mixed dried herbs
1⅔ cups milk
Salt and freshly ground black pepper
1 pound large dried pasta shells
Freshly grated Parmesan cheese,
   to serve

1 Heat 2 tablespoons oil in a large saucepan. Add the onion, garlic, and celery and cook for 10 minutes. Add the bacon and ground beef and cook, stirring, over a high heat for 3–4 minutes until the beef has browned.

2 Stir in the chopped tomatoes, tomato paste, herbs, and 1 cup of the milk. Cover and simmer the sauce for 40 minutes.

3 Add the remaining milk and simmer for a further 45 minutes. Taste and season with salt and pepper. Add a little water or broth if the sauce becomes very thick during cooking.

4 Preheat the oven to 350°F. Cook the pasta in a large pan of boiling salted water according to the instructions on the packet. Drain and toss in the remaining oil. Let cool a little, then arrange the shells in a large baking dish and fill with the bolognese sauce. Cook in the oven for 15 minutes. Serve with grated Parmesan cheese.

Beef Stew

with Herb Dumplings

Serves 6

½ cup all-purpose flour

Salt and freshly ground black pepper,
   to taste

3¼ pounds chuck steak or other
   stewing beef, cut into 2-inch cubes

About 4 tablespoons vegetable oil

2 large onions, thinly sliced

1 cup fruity red wine

2 cups beef broth or water

½ cup tomato ketchup

2 cloves garlic, finely chopped

2 bay leaves

1 large bouquet garni

2–3 carrots, cut into ½-inch pieces

1 pound butternut or acorn squash, cut
   into chunks

9 ounces pearl onions, peeled

1–2 tablespoons chopped parsley, to
   garnish

For the herb dumplings

1⅓ cups all-
   purpose flour

1½ teaspoons
   baking powder

½ teaspoon salt

⅓ cup beef suet, or vegetable
   shortening, grated

3–4 tablespoons finely chopped mixed
   fresh herbs, such as parsley, thyme
   sage, dill, and chives

4–6 tablespoons milk

Menu

*Beef Stew with
Herb Dumplings*

~

*Maple-baked
Acorn Squash
(p.189)*

~

*Fava Beans
with Prosciutto
(p.180)*

1 Put the flour in a plastic bag and season with salt and pepper. Working in small batches, put a few cubes of beef in the bag, twist the bag closed and shake to coat the meat evenly. Transfer the meat to a plate and continue to coat the remainder.

2 Heat the oil in a large, heavy-based saucepan over a medium-high heat. Working in batches, brown the beef cubes evenly on all sides, about 7 minutes for each batch. Transfer to a plate and continue until all the beef is browned.

continued on page 74

3 Add a little more oil, if necessary, then add the sliced onions. Cook for about 5 minutes, stirring, until softened. If you like a thicker stew, sprinkle over any remaining flour and cook for about 2 minutes, stirring to scrape up any browned bits from the bottom of the pan. Gradually whisk in the wine, broth or water, ketchup, garlic, bay leaves, and bouquet garni, and season to taste.

4 Bring to a boil, skimming off any foam that rises to the surface. Return the beef to the pan, reduce the heat to medium-low and simmer, covered, for 1½–1¾ hours, stirring occasionally, until the meat is almost tender. After simmering for 1 hour, stir in the carrots; and, after 1¼–1½ hours, stir in the butternut squash.

5 To prepare the dumplings, sift the flour, baking powder, and salt into a large bowl. Stir in the suet, mixed herbs, and a little pepper. Add the milk, little by little, stirring to make a soft dough.

6 Remove the bouquet garni from the stew and stir in the pearl onions. Using a large spoon, drop 8 large or 12 small balls of dumpling mixture into the stew. Simmer for about 20 minutes, covered, until the dumplings are puffed and slightly firm to the touch.

Easy Burritos

Serves 4-6

4–6 large flour tortillas
2–3 tablespoons vegetable oil
1 onion, coarsely chopped
1 red or green bell pepper, seeded and
  chopped
1 clove garlic, crushed
1½ pounds boneless pork loin or
  skinless, boneless chicken breast,
  thinly sliced
½ teaspoon crushed dried chiles, or to
  taste
½ teaspoon ground cumin
Salt and freshly ground black pepper
10-ounce can sweetcorn kernels,
  drained
2 ripe tomatoes, chopped
Bottled taco sauce, sliced avocado,
  sliced red onion, shredded iceberg
  lettuce, grated cheddar cheese, sour
  cream and fresh cilantro leaves, to
  serve

Menu

Easy Burritos
~
*Mexican Pot Beans
(p.190)*
~
*Old-fashioned
Cornbread
(p.210)*
~
*Tomato Salsa
(p.162)*

1 Preheat the oven to 350°F. Wrap the tortillas tightly in aluminum foil and heat in the oven for about 15 minutes.

2 Meanwhile, heat 2 tablespoons of oil in a large skillet or wok over a medium-high heat. Add the onion, pepper, and garlic and stir-fry 2–3 minutes until beginning to soften. Transfer to a plate and set aside.

3 Add the remaining oil, the pork or chicken, crushed chiles, and cumin and stir-fry for about 3 minutes. Season with salt and pepper and return the cooked vegetables to the pan. Add the sweetcorn and tomatoes and cook 2–3 minutes longer until heated through.

4 Lay the warm tortillas on a surface and divide the mixture evenly among them, placing it near one edge. Top with the chosen accompaniments. Fold the edge nearest the filling over just enough to cover the filling. Fold the two sides over to form an envelope shape.

Roast Rib of Beef

with Caramelized Shallots

Serves 4

6 pounds beef rib roast
2 tablespoons bacon fat or
   vegetable oil
Salt and freshly ground black pepper
6 fresh thyme sprigs
1 pound shallots, peeled and left whole
2 tablespoons sugar

For the sauce
1 tablespoon flour
1 cup red wine
2 cups beef broth

1 Preheat the oven to 400°F. Put the beef in a large roasting pan and spoon over the bacon fat or oil. Season well with salt and pepper and lay the thyme sprigs over the meat. Roast in the oven for 1 hour.

2 Meanwhile, bring a saucepan of water to a boil. Add the shallots and simmer for 15 minutes, then drain well.

3 Remove the beef from the oven. Arrange the shallots around the beef. Sprinkle the sugar over the shallots and return to the oven for a further 30 minutes, basting and turning the shallots after 15 minutes. Transfer the beef and shallots to a warm plate and leave to rest for at least 15 minutes.

4 For the sauce, pour off all but 2 tablespoons of the bacon fat or oil from the roasting pan, add the flour and cook on the stovetop for 1–2 minutes. Add the wine, stirring well to prevent lumps, then increase the heat a little and boil the liquid for 3–4 minutes to reduce and thicken.

5 Add the beef broth, reduce the heat and simmer for 10 minutes. Taste and season with salt and pepper.

Menu

*Rib Roast
with Caramelized
Shallots*
~
*Leek & Potato
Gratin (p.169)*
~
*Pumpkin Pie
(p.220)*

Old-fashioned Meatloaf

Serves 6

2 tablespoons vegetable oil, plus extra
for oiling
1 large onion, finely chopped
1 carrot, grated
2 cloves garlic, chopped
2 pounds ground beef
3/4 cup fresh white bread crumbs
2 eggs, lightly beaten
1/2 teaspoon dried thyme
2–4 tablespoons finely chopped
parsley
1 tablespoon Worcestershire sauce
2/3 cup tomato ketchup, plus extra for
glazing
Salt and freshly ground black pepper

1 Heat the oil in a skillet. Add the onion and carrot and cook for about 5 minutes, stirring frequently, until the vegetables begin to soften. Stir in the garlic and cook for a further 1 minute. Remove from the heat and let cool.

2 Preheat the oven to 350°F and lightly oil a 9 x 5 x 3-inch loaf pan. Combine the beef, bread crumbs and cooled vegetable mixture in a large bowl. Add the eggs, thyme, parsley, Worcestershire sauce, ketchup, and salt and pepper, then use a fork or your hands to mix the ingredients lightly together until just blended. Do not overwork the mixture or the meatloaf will be too compact and dry.

3 Spoon the mixture into the prepared pan, pressing gently to smooth the top. Bake for about 1¼ hours, or until the edges begin to shrink from the sides of the pan. About 10 minutes before the meatloaf is done, brush the top with about 2 tablespoons ketchup to give it a glaze.

4 Set aside to cool for about 10 minutes, covered loosely with foil. Pour off any excess juices, if you like, before leaving the meatloaf to cool. To serve, turn out on to a dish or plate and cut into slices. Alternatively, slice the meatloaf from the pan.

Menu

Old-fashioned
Meatloaf
~
Succotash
(p.173)
~
Texas Pilaf
(p.203)
~
Apple Cake Bars
(p.241)

Beef Stew with Star Anise

Serves 4–6

3 tablespoons vegetable oil

2 cloves garlic, crushed

1-inch piece fresh ginger, peeled and finely chopped

3 onions, finely sliced

2 pounds boneless beef (sirloin), cut into 1-inch cubes

3 tablespoons hoisin sauce

3 tablespoons light soy sauce

4 whole star anise

1 tablespoon mild honey or sugar

2 tablespoons rice wine or sherry

4 carrots, peeled and cut into 1-inch slices on the diagonal

Salt and freshly ground black pepper

1 tablespoon fresh chopped cilantro, to garnish

Steamed bok choy and rice, to serve

1 Heat the oil in a heavy-based skillet or casserole. Add the garlic, ginger, and onions and sauté over a high heat until golden brown.

2 Add the beef and brown on all sides. Pour over enough water to cover and stir in the hoisin and soy sauces, the star anise, honey or sugar, and rice wine or sherry. Simmer for 1½ hours, stirring from time to time to prevent sticking. Check the liquid level, adding more water if necessary.

3 Add the carrots and cook for a further 30 minutes, or until the meat and carrots are tender. Season to taste with salt and pepper.

4 Transfer to a serving dish, garnish with chopped cilantro, and serve with steamed bok choy and rice.

Menu

Beef Stew with Star Anise

~

Mango Ice Cream (p.216)

Braised Lamb Shanks
with Mirepoix Vegetables

Serves 4

1 tablespoon olive oil
4 lamb shanks
2 carrots, cut into very fine strips
3 ribs celery, cut into very fine strips
1 large onion, finely chopped
2 cloves garlic, finely chopped
2 cups red wine
1 cup lamb stock or chicken broth
1 tablespoon tomato paste
2 bay leaves
2 fresh rosemary sprigs
Salt and freshly ground black pepper

Tip
Mirepoix vegetables—diced carrot, onion, and celery—are perfect for enhancing soups, stews, and broth.

1 Preheat the oven to 300°F. Heat the oil in a large casserole and brown the lamb shanks all over for about 10 minutes. Transfer to a plate.

2 Add the vegetables to the casserole and fry for about 15 minutes until they start to take on a little color. Return the lamb shanks to the casserole and pour the wine and stock or broth over them. Add the tomato paste, bay leaves, and rosemary and season well with salt and pepper.

3 Bring to a boil, cover with a lid and cook in the oven for 3-3 1/2 hours. Turn the meat occasionally during cooking.

Menu

Braised Lamb Shanks with Mirepoix Vegetables

~

Duchesse Potatoes (p.166)

~

Stove-top Rice Pudding with Dried Fruit (p.245)

Tagine
with Prunes & Almonds

Serves 6

2³/₄ pounds boneless lean lamb, cut
   into 1¹/₂-inch cubes
¹/₄ cup *ras el hanout* or curry spice mix
¹/₂ cup water
¹/₂ cup olive oil
4 onions, halved and sliced
3 cinnamon sticks
1 large white turnip, cut into
   ³/₄-inch slices
12 ounces prunes
3 cloves garlic, crushed
Salt and freshly ground black pepper
1 cup toasted whole blanched almonds
2 tablespoons fresh chopped cilantro
   or parsley, to garnish
Steamed couscous, to serve

1 Put the lamb in a large non-metallic bowl. Blend the *ras el hanout* with the water and pour over the lamb. Mix well to coat each piece of meat. Marinate for at least 3 hours in the refrigerator.

2 Heat the oil in a heavy-based skillet or casserole. Add the onions and sauté over a high heat until they start to brown. Add the meat and cook until the pieces are brown on all sides.

3 Pour over enough water to cover, then add the cinnamon sticks and turnip. Simmer uncovered, for 30 minutes, stirring occasionally so that the meat doesn't stick to the bottom of the pan. Add more water if necessary.

4 Stir in the prunes and garlic, cover the pan and simmer for 30 minutes until the meat is tender, stirring from time to time.

5 Season with salt and pepper. Sprinkle toasted almonds over the top, garnish with cilantro or parsley, and serve with steamed couscous.

Menu

Tagine with Prunes & Almonds

~

Chickpea & Tomato Salad (p.195)

~

Spiced Baked Apples (p.224)

Lamb Meatballs

with Buttermilk & Herb Dip

Makes about 40

3 tablespoons vegetable oil, plus extra
    for frying
2 onions, finely chopped
4 cloves garlic, crushed
2 tablespoons paprika
2 teaspoons dried thyme
2 teaspoons cinnamon
2 pounds ground lamb
2 tablespoons finely chopped fresh
    cilantro
Salt and freshly ground black pepper

For the buttermilk dip
1¼ cups buttermilk
1 teaspoon chopped fresh thyme
1 tablespoon snipped fresh chives

1 Heat the oil in a large skillet. Add the onions and garlic and cook for 10 minutes. Add the paprika, thyme, and cinnamon and cook for a further 1–2 minutes. Let cool completely.

2 Mix the onion mixture into the lamb, then add the cilantro, and season well with salt and pepper. (To test the level of seasoning, cook just a nugget of the mixture.)

3 Shape the mixture into 40 small meatballs. Heat a little oil in a large skillet and cook the meatballs for 10–12 minutes, turning them halfway through cooking.

4 For the dip, mix the buttermilk and herbs together in a bowl. Taste and season with salt and pepper.

5 Serve the meatballs warm with toothpicks for your guests to dunk the meatballs into the buttermilk dip.

Menu

Lamb Meatballs with
Buttermilk & Herb Dip
~
Waldorf Salad (p.196)
~
Bacon & Caramelized
Onion Rolls (p.211)
~
Meringues with Cream
& Blueberries (p.223)

Papaya Lamb Kabobs

Serves 6

2 pounds boneless lamb, cut into
   1-inch cubes
12 pearl onions
2 green bell peppers, cored, seeded,
   and cut into 1-inch squares
1 red bell pepper, cored, seeded, and
   cut into 1-inch squares
Salt and freshly ground black pepper

For the marinade
1 small ripe papaya
Juice of 2 limes
1 teaspoon garam masala
1 teaspoon ground coriander
2 tablespoons light olive oil
$\frac{1}{4}$ cup plain yogurt

1 Make the marinade. Cut the papaya in half,
spoon out and discard the black seeds, then
scrape the flesh into a blender or food processor.
Add the remaining ingredients and process until
smooth. Spoon into a shallow glass dish, add the
lamb cubes and mix well. Cover and leave to
marinate in the refrigerator for 2–3 hours,
stirring occasionally.

Menu

*Papaya
Lamb Kabobs*
~
*Stir-fried Brown
Rice & Vegetables
(p.202)*

2 Preheat the broiler to medium. Put the
unpeeled onions in a saucepan and pour over
enough cold water to cover. Bring to a boil and boil
for 4 minutes, then drain. When cool enough to
handle, slip off the skins.

3 Drain the lamb cubes, reserving the marinade.
Thread them on to 12 metal skewers,
alternating them with the onions and pepper
squares. Season well with salt and pepper.

4 Cook the kabobs under the broiler or on
the grill for 15–20 minutes, turning them
occasionally and basting them with the marinade
during the first ten minutes of cooking.

Kofta

Serves 6

1 pound ground beef
1 pound ground lamb
2 onions, finely chopped
1 tablespoon paprika
1 tablespoon coriander seeds
1 teaspoon salt
$\frac{1}{2}$ teaspoon freshly ground black pepper
1 egg
$\frac{1}{2}$ cup fresh bread crumbs
3 tablespoons water
Butter, for greasing

For the tomato sauce

3 tablespoons olive oil
1 onion, finely chopped
6 ripe tomatoes, skinned, seeded
    and chopped
1 tablespoon ras el hanout or
    curry powder
1 teaspoon ground cumin
1 teaspoon coriander seeds
1 cinnamon stick
1 teaspoon sugar
$\frac{1}{2}$ cup water
Salt and freshly ground black pepper
2 tablespoons toasted sesame seeds,
    to garnish

Menu

Kofta
~
*Spiced Zucchini
(p.185)*
~
*Chilled Tangerine
& Lemon Mousse
(p.233)*

1 Mix the beef and lamb together in a large bowl. Add the onions, paprika, coriander seeds, salt, and pepper. Stir in the egg, bread crumbs, and the 3 tablespoons water until well mixed. Chill for about 3 hours.

2 Preheat the oven to 425°F and grease a baking dish.

3 Shape spoonfuls of the meat mixture into walnut-sized balls, and arrange in the baking dish. Bake for 15 minutes, or until lightly browned.

4 To make the tomato sauce, heat the oil in a large saucepan. Add the onions and cook over a high heat until transparent. Add the tomatoes, ras el hanout, spices, and sugar, and stir in the $\frac{1}{2}$ cup water. Simmer for 20 minutes. Add 2 teaspoons salt and $\frac{1}{2}$ teaspoon pepper.

5 Add the meatballs and any juices to the sauce and simmer gently for about 30 minutes. Remove the cinnamon stick and adjust the seasoning. Transfer to a serving dish. Sprinkle with toasted sesame seeds.

Roast Leg of Lamb

Serves 6–8

1 leg of lamb (weigh once prepared for
  cooking)
2–3 cloves garlic, sliced
2–3 fresh rosemary sprigs
Salt and freshly ground black pepper
1 cup red wine
1¼ cups lamb stock or water

1 Preheat the oven to 425°F. Using a small, sharp knife, make about 8-10 deep incisions in the meat. Into each incision, insert a slice of garlic along with a few leaves of rosemary (you can usually pull off small bunches of leaves attached at the stem end). Season the lamb well all over with salt and pepper. Transfer to a large roasting pan.

2 Roast the lamb for 25 minutes per pound plus 25 minutes for medium, 30 minutes per pound plus 30 minutes for well done. When finished, remove the meat from the roasting pan to a carving board. Let rest for 10–15 minutes.

3 To make the gravy, remove as much fat as possible from the roasting pan, using a metal spoon. Place the pan on the hob over a medium heat. When sizzling, pour in the red wine. Using a spoon or whisk, scrape up any residue in the bottom of the pan. Allow the wine to simmer rapidly until reduced to a syrupy consistency. Now add the stock or water (if you have any water from cooking vegetables or potatoes, use that). Bring to a boil and simmer rapidly until reduced by about half. Taste and add a little seasoning. If the flavor is not concentrated enough, continue reducing a little more. Strain the gravy into a gravy boat. Slice the meat and serve with the gravy.

Menu

Roast Leg of Lamb
~
*Provençal
Ratatouille (p.155)*
~
*Luxury Mashed
Potatoes (p.166)*
~
*Double-crust Apple Pie
(p.228)*

Baked Lasagne

Menu

Baked Lasagne
~
Braised Fennel (p.177)
~
Chocolate Mousse
(p.232)

Serves 8

2 tablespoons olive oil
1 onion, finely chopped
2 cloves garlic, crushed
1 pound minced beef
Two 14-ounce cans plum tomatoes
14-ounce can tomato sauce
2–3 tablespoons tomato paste
Salt and freshly ground black pepper
1 tablespoon chopped fresh oregano
1 tablespoon chopped fresh thyme
1 teaspoon dried red pepper flakes
1 bay leaf
About 14 fresh or dried lasagne sheets
2 eggs, lightly beaten
16 ounces ricotta cheese
2 tablespoons chopped fresh parsley
   or basil
16 ounces mozzarella cheese
Freshly grated Parmesan cheese

1 Heat the oil in a large saucepan over medium heat. Add the onion and cook until just soft. Add the garlic and beef and cook until browned. Stir in the tomatoes, tomato sauce, and tomato paste, then season. Add the oregano, thyme, pepper flakes, and bay leaf. Bring to a boil (squash the tomatoes to break them up.) Reduce the heat to low, partially cover and simmer for 45 minutes, stirring occasionally, until the sauce is slightly reduced. Remove the bay leaf.

2 For fresh lasagne, no pre-cooking is necessary. For dried lasagne, bring a large, deep skillet half-filled with salted water to a boil over a high heat. Working in batches, cook the lasagne for 2–3 minutes. Drain and lay out to dry on a paper towel.

3 Preheat the oven to 375°F. Beat the eggs and ricotta together in a bowl until blended, season and stir in the parsley or basil.

4 Spoon enough meat sauce into a deep baking dish about 9 x 13 inches just to cover the bottom. Cover with a layer of lasagne. Spread a third of the ricotta mixture on top and sprinkle with a little mozzarella, then cover with a layer of meat sauce. Continue the layers, ending with meat sauce and mozzarella. Sprinkle with grated Parmesan. Transfer the dish to a baking sheet and bake for 45–55 minutes, or until bubbling and crisp around the edges. Let stand for 5–10 minutes before serving.

- Home-smoked Salmon

- Atlantic Spiced Salmon with New Potato & Spring Onion Salad

- New England Clam Chowder

- Fish & Chips

- Crab Louis

- Swordfish Kabobs with Lemon Herb Mayonnaise

- Fish Caldine

- Beer-battered Shrimp

- Grapefruit, Shrimp & Avocado Salad

- Shrimp Jambalaya

- Marinated Shrimp with Dill Mayonnaise

- Poached Whole Salmon

- Green Curry with Shrimp

- Porgy with Garlic & Coriander Butter

- Crispy Fish Cakes

- Sweet Chile Salmon

- Tuna Noodle Casserole

- Tuna Melts

- Grilled Tuna with Warm Bean Salad

- Baked Fish with Celeriac

- Fish Stick Sandwiches with Mayonnaise

- Roast Cod with Fried Gremolata Bread Crumbs

- New England Fishballs

- Smoked Trout Terrine with Cucumber Salad

- Harissa-coated Monkfish

CHAPTER THREE

FISH & SHELLFISH

Home-smoked Salmon

Serves 6

1 cup rice
8 fresh rosemary sprigs
Six 6-ounce salmon fillets
2 teaspoons vegetable oil
Salt and freshly ground black pepper

Menu

*Home-smoked
Salmon*
~
*Roast Peppers
with Mozzarella
(p.154)*
~
*New England
Blueberry Pancakes
(p.226)*

1 Preheat the oven to 400°F. Line a wok with aluminum foil and pour in the rice. Arrange the rosemary on top of the rice. Sprinkle with a little water and fit a round wire rack in the wok. Heat the wok until smoking, then put the salmon fillets on the wire rack. Cover tightly and smoke for 5 minutes.

2 Remove the salmon to a roasting pan and brush it with oil. Season with salt and pepper and cook in the oven for 5 minutes. Rest for a few minutes and serve the salmon warm.

Atlantic Spiced Salmon

with New Potato & Spring Onion Salad

Serves 8

8 Atlantic salmon fillets,
  about 6–8 ounces each
4 tablespoons paprika
4 tablespoons dried oregano
2 cloves garlic, crushed
½ teaspoon cayenne pepper
½ cup olive oil
Salt and freshly ground black pepper

For the salad
4 pounds new potatoes, scrubbed
⅔ cup vegetable oil
2 tablespoons lemon juice
15 scallions, finely chopped
¼ cup chopped fresh mint

1 Put the salmon fillets in a large non-metallic dish. Mix the paprika, oregano, garlic, cayenne, olive oil, and a few grinds of pepper together in a large bowl. Pour the marinade over the salmon and work it into the flesh with your hands. Marinate in the refrigerator for 2 hours.

2 Meanwhile, for the salad, put the potatoes in a saucepan of salted water, bring to a boil and until tender. Mix the oil and lemon juice together in a bowl. Drain the potatoes, then return them to the pan and pour the dressing over. Toss well, then cover and leave the potatoes to steep in the dressing for 30 minutes.

3 Preheat the oven to 425°F. Put the salmon in a large roasting pan, season well with salt and roast in the oven for 12–15 minutes. Set aside for 5 minutes before serving.

4 Transfer the potatoes to a serving dish and stir in the onions and mint, then serve with the salmon.

Menu

Atlantic Spiced Salmon with New Potato & Spring Onion Salad

~

Sticky Toffee Pudding (p.225)

New England

Clam Chowder

Serves 4

Menu

New England Clam Chowder

~

Bacon & Caramelized Onion Rolls (p.211)

3 pounds fresh clams
¼ stick (2 tablespoons) butter
1 onion, finely chopped
3 slices bacon, finely chopped
2 medium-sized potatoes, peeled and diced
4 fresh thyme sprigs
1 bay leaf
2½ cups milk
Salt and freshly ground black pepper

Tip
Served with hot crusty bread and followed by fruit or cheese, this will make a meal in itself for lunch or supper.

1 Wash and scrub the clams. Discard any that refuse to close after a sharp tap. Pour enough water to come up to ½ inch in a large saucepan and add the clams. Cover with a tight-fitting lid and bring to a boil. Cook for 2 minutes then drain, reserving 1¼ cups of the cooking liquid. Remove the clams from their shells, discarding any that are shut.

2 Melt the butter in a large saucepan. Add the onion, bacon, and potatoes and fry for 5 minutes.

3 Add the thyme sprigs, bay leaf, and milk. Pour in the reserved liquid and simmer the soup until the potatoes are on the point of breaking up, about 20–25 minutes. Remove the thyme and bay leaf. Season well with salt and pepper and stir in the clams. Simmer for 1 minute, to heat the soup through and serve.

Fish & Chips

Serves 6–8

Menu

Fish & Chips

~

*Caramel
Ice Cream (p.217)*

1 tablespoon fresh yeast
1¼ cups beer
1¾ cups all-purpose flour
2 teaspoons salt
2 pounds russet potatoes
Vegetable oil, for deep-frying
4 thick pieces cod fillet, about 6 ounces
   each, preferably from the head end
Salt and freshly ground black pepper
Fresh parsley sprigs, to garnish

1 For the batter, cream the yeast with a little of the beer to a smooth paste. Gradually stir in the rest of the beer. Sift the flour and salt into a bowl, make a well in the center and add the yeast mixture. Gradually whisk to a smooth batter. Cover and leave at room temperature for 1 hour until foamy and thick.

2 For English-style French fries, cut the potatoes into chips about ½ inch thick. Heat a large saucepan half filled with oil for deep-frying to 275°F, or until a cube of bread browns in 1 minute. Cook the chips in two batches for about 5 minutes, or until they are cooked through but not browned. Drain on paper towels and set aside.

3 Increase the heat to 325°F, or until a cube of bread browns in 45 seconds. Season the fish generously with salt and pepper and then dip into the batter. Deep-fry two pieces at a time for 7-8 minutes until deep golden brown and the fish is cooked through. Lift out, drain on paper towels and keep warm while you cook the remaining fish pieces. Keep the fish warm while you finish the chips.

4 Increase the heat to 375°F or until a cube of bread browns in 30 seconds. Fry the chips again, in two batches, for 2–3 minutes until crisp and golden. Drain on paper towels and sprinkle with salt. Garnish the fish and chips with parsley sprigs, and serve with lemon wedges and mayonnaise.

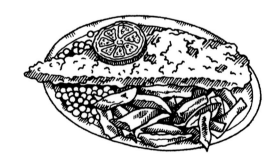

Crab Louis

Serves 4

1 head Boston or butterhead lettuce,
   leaves separated, washed and dried
16–24 ounce-lump crabmeat,
   picked over
4 hard-boiled eggs, halved
8 cherry tomatoes, halved
20 black olives, preferably niçoise or
   herb-dried
1 tablespoon chopped fresh dill,
   to garnish

For the dressing
1 cup mayonnaise
1 tablespoon lemon juice
½ small onion, grated
½ green bell pepper, seeded
   and finely chopped
¼ cup sweet or hot chile sauce, or
   to taste
1 teaspoon Worcestershire sauce

Menu

Crab Louis
~
*Spanish Omelet
(p.136)*
~
*Chocolate Mousse
(p.232)*

1 To make the dressing, put the mayonnaise in a bowl and stir in the lemon juice, onion, pepper, chile and Worcestershire sauces until well blended. Set aside.

2 Arrange the lettuce leaves on 4 plates. Mound equal amounts of crabmeat in the middle and arrange the hard-boiled eggs and tomato halves around the crab.

3 Sprinkle the olives over the top and spoon over some of the dressing. Sprinkle with dill to garnish and serve the remaining dressing separately.

Swordfish Kabobs with

Lemon Herb Mayonnaise

Serves 4

For the mayonnaise
1 egg yolk
Salt and freshly ground black pepper
1 tablespoon white wine vinegar
½ teaspoon Dijon mustard
¾ cup olive oil

For the flavoring
2 teaspoons grated lemon zest
1 tablespoon chopped fresh tarragon
1 tablespoon chopped capers
1 tablespoon chopped fresh parsley

For the kabobs
1 pound swordfish steak, cut into bite-sized pieces
2 red onions, cut into 6 wedges
2 limes, each cut into wedges
2 tablespoons olive oil
Zest of 1 lime
1 teaspoon fresh thyme leaves
2 tablespoons maple syrup
Boiled new potatoes, to serve

Menu

Swordfish Kabobs with Lemon Herb Mayonnaise
~
Classic Healthy Coleslaw (p. 191)

1 For the mayonnaise, whisk the egg yolk, salt and pepper, vinegar, and mustard together until they thicken slightly.

2 Add the olive oil a drop at a time whisking continuously. When the sauce begins to thicken and lighten, start adding the oil in a thin, steady stream, whisking continuously.

3 When all the oil has been added, taste for seasoning then stir in the lemon zest, tarragon, capers, and parsley. Set aside.

4 Put the swordfish, red onion, and lime wedges into a bowl and toss in the olive oil, lime zest, thyme leaves, and maple syrup. Chill 2-3 hours.

5 Preheat the broiler. Thread the fish, lime wedges, and red onion onto 8 skewers and cook under the hot broiler for 5-6 minutes, turning often until starting to color on the outside. Serve the kabobs with a spoonful of the sauce and boiled new potatoes.

Fish Caldine

Serves 4–6

1-inch piece fresh root ginger, peeled
1 teaspoon ground cumin
1 teaspoon ground turmeric
1 clove garlic, peeled
Salt
14-ounce can unsweetened coconut
  milk
4 tablespoons vegetable oil
2 pounds firm-fleshed white fish, either
  whole or in fillets (scored three times
  on each side if using whole fish)
1 onion, finely chopped
1 fresh green chile, finely chopped
1 tablespoon whole fresh cilantro
  leaves
1 chile, sliced lengthwise, to garnish
1 lime, cut into wedges, to serve

1 Put the ginger, cumin, turmeric, garlic, and
1 teaspoon salt in a food processor and process
to a smooth purée. With the motor running, add the
coconut milk and process until smooth. Set aside.

2 Heat 2 tablespoons of the oil in a heavy-based
skillet. Add the fish and sear for 2 minutes on

each side. Carefully remove the fish and set aside. In
the same pan, add the remaining 2 tablespoons oil
and fry the onion and finely chopped chile together
over a high heat until the onion is soft and
transparent. Return the fish to the pan. Add the
coconut milk mixture and reduce the heat.

3 Simmer gently for 10–15 minutes, basting the
fish with the coconut mixture frequently, until
most of the liquid has been absorbed. Adjust the
seasoning.

4 Transfer the fish to a serving dish and sprinkle
with cilantro leaves. Garnish with sliced green
chile and serve with lime wedges for squeezing over.

Menu

Fish Caldine
~
Braised Fennel
(p.177)
~
Latkes
(p.171)
~
Cherry Clafoutis
(p.243)

Beer-battered Shrimp

Serves 4–6

1½–2 pounds large raw shrimp, peeled
and deveined, with tails if possible
Vegetable oil, for deep-frying

For the batter
1 cup all-purpose flour
1½ teaspoons salt
¾–1 cup beer
Lemon and lime wedges and fresh
parsley sprigs, to garnish

Menu

*Beer-battered
Shrimp*

~

*Old-fashioned
English Chips
(p.164)*

1 Rinse the shrimp and dry them well with paper towels.

2 For the batter, sift the flour into a bowl and stir in the salt. Using a fork, gradually stir in the beer—do not overmix the batter as a few lumps of flour will not matter.

3 Heat the oil for deep-frying to 375°F over medium-high heat. Using your fingers or tongs and working in batches, dip the shrimp into the batter and then drop them into the hot oil. Cook for about 1 minute, until crisp and golden, turning once. Drain on paper towels and keep hot until all the prawns are battered and cooked.

4 Arrange the shrimp in a napkin-lined basket or bowl and garnish with lemon and lime wedges and parsley sprigs.

Grapefruit, Shrimp & Avocado Salad

Serves 4

1 clove garlic, peeled
Grated zest and juice of 1 lemon
2 tablespoons olive oil
1 pound raw peeled shrimp
2 grapefruit
2 avocados
Small bunch of fresh chives

Tip

To stop a cut avocado from discoloring, brush the cut surfaces with lemon juice.

Menu

Grapefruit, Shrimp & Avocado Salad

~

Onion Quiche
(p.139)

~

Chocolate-covered Doughnuts
(p.238)

1 Pound the garlic in a mortar and pestle with the lemon zest and juice and 1 tablespoon of the oil. Spoon into a bowl and add the shrimps. Stir and leave to marinate for 30 minutes.

2 Peel and segment the grapefruit with a serrated fruit knife and arrange in a salad bowl. Halve the avocados, remove the pits and peel away the skin. Thinly slice and carefully arrange among the grapefruit segments.

3 Heat the remaining oil in a skillet. Add the shrimp, and fry for 3–4 minutes until firm and pink all over. Let cool then spoon over the salad. Snip the chives with a pair of kitchen scissors and scatter over the salad. Chill until ready to serve.

Shrimp Jambalaya

Serves 6

2 tablespoons vegetable oil
2 medium onions, roughly chopped
1 green bell pepper, seeded and
   roughly chopped
2 ribs celery, roughly chopped
3 cloves garlic, finely chopped
2 teaspoons paprika
10 ounces skinless, boneless chicken
   breasts, chopped
3½ ounces andouille or chorizo
   sausage, chopped
3 large tomatoes, skinned and chopped
1 pound long-grain rice
2¼ cups hot chicken or fish broth
1 teaspoon dried oregano
2 fresh bay leaves
12 jumbo shrimp
4 scallions, finely chopped
2 tablespoons chopped fresh parsley
Salt and freshly ground black pepper

1 Heat the oil in a large skillet. Add the onions, pepper, celery, and garlic and cook for 8-10 minutes until all the vegetables have softened. Add the paprika and cook for a further 30 seconds. Add the chicken and sausage and cook for 8-10 minutes until lightly browned. Add the tomatoes to the pan. Cook for 2-3 minutes until they collapse.

2 Add the rice to the pan and stir well. Pour in the hot broth, oregano, and bay leaves and stir well. Cover and simmer for 10 minutes over a very low heat.

3 Add the shrimp and stir well. Cover again and cook for a further 6-8 minutes until the rice is tender and the shrimp are cooked through.

4 Stir in the scallions and parsley and season to taste with salt and pepper. Serve immediately.

> **Menu**
>
> *Shrimp
> Jambalaya*
> ~
> *Spinach
> with Paneer
> (p.151)*
> ~
> *Apple Sauce Sundae
> (p.236)*

Marinated Shrimp
with Dill Mayonnaise

Serves 8

40 large raw peeled shrimp
2 cloves garlic, crushed
Juice and grated zest of 2 limes
1 fresh or dried red chile, seeded and
   very finely chopped

For the dill mayonnaise
2 egg yolks
1 teaspoon mustard powder
2 teaspoons white wine vinegar
Pinch of salt
1 cup peanut or vegetable oil
2 teaspoons sour cream
1 tablespoon chopped fresh dill

1 Put the shrimp in a shallow, non-metallic dish. Mix the garlic, lime juice, zest, and chile together in a bowl. Pour the marinade over the shrimp. Mix well and marinate for 1 hour.

2 To make the mayonnaise, put the egg yolks, mustard powder, vinegar, and salt in a mixing bowl. Using an electric mixer, beat in the oil, drop by drop at first. When half of the oil has been added, pour in the remaining oil in a thin, steady stream, whisking continuously. If the mayonnaise becomes very thick, dilute with 1 tablespoon warm water.

3 Stir the sour cream and dill into the mayonnaise. Chill until ready to serve.

4 Put the shrimp in a steamer (you may need to do this in batches) and steam for 3–4 minutes until they turn pink and firm. Serve chilled or at room temperature with the dill mayonnaise.

Menu

*Marinated
Shrimp with Dill
Mayonnaise*
~
*Parsley &
Leek Frittata
(p.135)*
~
*Peanut Butter
Brownies
(p.240)*

Poached Whole Salmon

Serves 8–10

2 carrots, sliced
2 leeks, sliced
2 medium onions, sliced
1 teaspoon black peppercorns
1 bouquet garni
2 cups dry white wine
2 teaspoons white wine vinegar
2 cups cold water
1 whole salmon, about 4½ pounds in
   weight, scaled and washed
Boiled new potatoes, to serve

1 To make the court-bouillon, put the carrots,
leeks, onions, peppercorns, bouquet garni, wine,
and wine vinegar into a large saucepan along with
the water. Bring slowly to a boil and simmer gently
for 20 minutes. Remove from the heat and let cool.

2 Put the salmon into a fish kettle or large
saucepan. Pour over the court-bouillon, adding
water if necessary to cover the fish. Bring slowly up
to a simmer and cook for 15 minutes. Remove from
the heat and leave in the liquid until cold.

3 Lift the fish from the poaching liquid and onto a
large chopping board. Remove the fish head and
discard. Carefully remove the skin from the

uppermost section of
the fish. Slide a knife
between the spine
and bones to remove
the fillet in one piece
if possible. Remove
the bones and
replace the fillet.

4 Carefully flip the
fish and repeat,
first removing the
skin, then the fillet. You now have a boneless
cooked salmon. Carefully transfer to a serving
platter. Serve with mayonnaise and boiled
new potatoes.

Menu

*Poached
Whole Salmon*
~
*Spinach Roulade
(p.157)*
~
*Boston Cream Pie
(p.244)*

Green Curry with Shrimp

Serves 4

For the green curry paste

5 fresh green chiles, seeded
  and chopped
2 teaspoons chopped fresh
  lemon grass,
1 large shallot, chopped
2 cloves garlic, chopped
1 teaspoon freshly grated ginger or
  galangal, if available
2 cilantro roots, chopped
½ teaspoon ground coriander
¼ teaspoon ground cumin
1 kaffir lime leaf, finely chopped
½ teaspoon salt

For the green curry paste

2 tablespoons vegetable oil
1 clove garlic, chopped
1 small eggplant, diced
½ cup coconut milk
2 tablespoons Thai fish sauce
1 teaspoon sugar
1 pound raw peeled tiger shrimp
½ cup fish stock
2 kaffir lime leaves, finely shredded
About 15 Thai basil leaves, or
  ordinary basil

1 To make the green curry paste, put all the ingredients into a blender or spice grinder and process to a fairly smooth paste, adding a little water if necessary. Alternatively, pound the ingredients using a mortar and pestle until fairly smooth. Set aside.

2 To make the curry, heat the oil in a skillet or wok until almost smoking and add the garlic. Fry until golden. Add the green curry paste that you have made and stir-fry a few seconds before adding the eggplant. Stir-fry for about 4–5 minutes until softened.

3 Add the coconut milk. Bring to a boil and stir until the cream thickens and curdles slightly. Add the fish sauce and sugar and stir well until combined.

4 Add the shrimp and stock. Simmer for 3–4 minutes, stirring occasionally, until the shrimp are just tender. Add the lime leaves and basil leaves and cook for a further minute.

Menu

*Green Curry
with Shrimp*
~
*Coconut Rice
(p.206)*
~
*Mango
Ice Cream
(p.216)*

Porgy with Garlic
& Cilantro Butter

Menu

*Porgy with
Garlic & Cilantro
Butter*

~

*Spinach Roulade
(p.157)*

~

*Pumpkin Pie
(p.220)*

Serves 4

1 tablespoon brown sugar
1 teaspoon freshly ground black
  pepper
1 teaspoon salt
4 porgies, or 2 red snapper, about
  4 pounds total weight
1 stick (8 tablespoons) unsalted butter,
  softened
2 cloves garlic, crushed
2 tablespoons chopped fresh cilantro
Juice and finely grated zest of 1 lemon
1 tablespoon dried red pepper flakes
Salt and freshly ground black pepper
Lemon wedges, to serve

1 Preheat the a gas grill to high direct heat. Mix the brown sugar, black pepper, and salt together. Rub the mixture into the skin of the fish. Set aside.

2 Beat the butter, garlic, cilantro, lemon zest, and pepper flakes together in a medium mixing bowl. Season to taste with salt and pepper. When thoroughly mixed, add the lemon juice and beat until incorporated. Scrape the mixture onto a large piece of parchment paper and, using the paper to help you, shape into a log. Enclose the butter in the paper and twist the ends together to seal. Chill in the refrigerator until needed.

3 Cook the fish over high direct heat for 8-12 minutes, turning once halfway through the cooking time, until the skin is crisp and golden and the flesh just flakes. Remove from the heat and transfer to serving plates (if using porgy) or cut into fillets (if using snapper).

4 Slice the butter thickly and put 1-2 slices on top of the fish. Serve immediately with the wedges of lemon.

Crispy Fish Cakes

Serves 4

Juice of ¹/₂ lemon
1¹/₄ pounds cod or other white fish,
   salmon or trout fillets or steaks
1 pound potatoes, cut into pieces
Salt and freshly ground black pepper
²/₃ stick (5 tablespoons) butter
1 onion, finely chopped
1 large egg
1 egg yolk
2 tablespoons chopped fresh dill,
   chives, or parsley, or a mixture
Dried bread crumbs, for coating
Vegetable oil, for frying
Fresh parsley or dill sprigs, to garnish

1 Bring a medium skillet half-filled with water to a boil. Add the lemon juice and 1 teaspoon salt. Add the fish and reduce the heat to low. Simmer until the fish is just cooked, spooning water over it to poach the top. Drain on paper towels and cool.

2 Flake the fish into a bowl, picking out any bones or skin. Lay plastic wrap on the surface of the fish to stop it drying out. Meanwhile, cook the potatoes in boiling salted water for 15 minutes, or until tender. Drain and return to the pan. Mash until smooth. Beat in 3 tablespoons butter and season.

3 Melt half the remaining butter in a small skillet over a medium heat. Add the onion and cook gently for about 7 minutes, or until softened. Stir into the mashed potato mixture.

4 Beat the egg, egg yolk, and chopped herbs into the potato mixture, then gently fold in the fish until well blended. Taste for seasoning and add a squeeze of lemon juice. Shape into 8 patties.

5 Put the bread crumbs in a plastic bag. Put each fish patty into the bag in turn and shake and turn to coat completely with bread crumbs. Arrange on a baking sheet and chill for at least 20 minutes.

6 Heat about a 2-inch depth of oil for frying in a large, heavy-based skillet. Add 1 tablespoon butter and heat over a medium-high heat until the butter is melted and sizzling, then swirl to blend the butter and oil. Add the fish cakes and cook for 8 minutes, or until golden brown on both sides, turning halfway through cooking. Drain on paper towels and serve garnished with the parsley or dill.

Menu

Crispy Fish Cakes
~
Waldorf Salad
(p.196)
~
Double-crust Apple Pie
(p.228)

Sweet Chile Salmon

Serves 4

1 tablespoon honey
2 small hot red chiles, seeded and
   finely chopped
Juice of 1 lime
2 tablespoons olive oil
4 salmon steaks, about 8 ounces each

For the salsa
3 cloves garlic, peeled
2 jalapeño chiles
3 long green chiles
1 ear fresh corn, husked
2 tablespoons olive oil
1 large tomato
Juice of 2 limes
2 tablespoons tequila
1 cup cooked black beans, drained
1 small red onion, finely chopped
3 tablespoons chopped fresh
   cilantro
Salt and freshly ground black pepper

1 Preheat a gas grill to high direct heat. Mix the honey, red chiles, lime juice, and 1 tablespoon oil in a bowl. Put the salmon steaks into a non-metallic dish and pour the marinade over. Cover and set aside for 30 minutes.

2 Meanwhile, to make the salsa, thread the garlic and jalapeños onto a metal skewer. Brush the garlic, jalapeños, long green chiles, and corn with oil. Grill the vegetables for 8-12 minutes, or until softened and charred. Transfer the chiles to a plastic bag and leave until cool enough to handle.

3 Chop the garlic. Peel the chiles and remove the stems and seeds. Chop the flesh. Seed and chop the tomato. Cut the kernels from the corn cobs with a serrated knife. Blend the tomato, jalapeños, garlic, lime juice, and tequila in a blender or food processor until fairly smooth, then transfer to a bowl. Add the remaining chopped chiles, corn kernels, black beans, red onion, and cilantro. Season, then cover and let stand until needed. Preheat the broiler if cooking indoors.

4 Lift the salmon from the marinade. Grill over high direct heat or under the broiler for 6-8 minutes, turning once and brushing occasionally with the marinade.

Menu

*Sweet Chile
Salmon*
~
*Braised Sugar Snaps
with Lettuce
(p.178)*
~
*Baked Alaska
Birthday Cake
(p.235)*

Tuna Noodle Casserole

Serves 6–8

¾ stick (6 tablespoons) butter
1 onion, finely chopped
2 ribs celery, thinly sliced
½ teaspoon dried thyme
¼ cup all-purpose flour
Salt and freshly ground black pepper
3 cups milk
½ cup sour cream (optional)
6 ounces mushrooms, sliced and
   lightly sautéed in butter
1¼ cups frozen peas, thawed
8 ounces egg noodles, cooked and
   drained
2 x 6½-ounce cans tuna, drained
¼ cup dried bread crumbs

1 Preheat the oven to 350°F. Melt 4 tablespoons of the butter in a large, heavy-based saucepan over a medium heat. Add the onion, celery, and thyme and cook, stirring frequently, for about 5 minutes, or until the vegetables are softened.

2 Stir in the flour and cook, stirring frequently, for about 2 minutes, or until well blended. Season with salt and pepper.

3 Gradually whisk in the milk and cook until the sauce thickens and begins to boil. Reduce the heat to low and simmer for about 10 minutes, stirring frequently. If the sauce becomes too thick, add a little more milk. Remove from the heat and stir in the sour cream.

4 Add the mushrooms, peas, and noodles, and flake in the tuna. Toss well to combine and turn into a large baking dish, then spread the mixture out evenly.

5 Melt the remaining butter in a small skillet over a medium heat. Add the bread crumbs and stir to coat completely, then sprinkle the mixture evenly over the casserole.

6 Cook in the oven for about 25 minutes, or until the top is crisp and golden and the casserole is bubbling. Serve immediately.

> **Menu**
>
> Tuna Noodle
> Casserole
> ~
> Sticky Toffee
> Pudding
> (p.225)

Tuna Melts

Makes about 40

20 slices white bread
²/₃ stick (5 tablespoons) butter, melted
13-ounce can tuna in oil, drained
    and flaked
¹/₂ cup mayonnaise
2 tablespoons snipped fresh chives
Grated zest of 2 lemons
1 cup grated cheddar cheese
Salt and freshly ground black pepper

Menu

Tuna Melts
~
Succotash
(p.173)
~
Apple Cake Bars
(p.241)

1 Preheat the oven to 350°F. Cut out rounds of bread with a 2-inch pastry cutter to make 40 rounds—you should get 2 rounds per slice of bread. (Use the trimmings to make bread crumbs.)

2 Lay the bread rounds on a baking sheet and brush with melted butter. Bake in the oven for 10 minutes until crisp and golden.

3 Mix the tuna with the remaining ingredients. Taste and season with salt and pepper. Place 1 heaped teaspoon of the tuna mixture on each round, making sure you spread the mixture to the edges of the bread so it doesn't burn when broiled. Preheat the broiler.

4 Put the rounds on a baking sheet and broil for 2–3 minutes until slightly brown and just beginning to melt. Serve warm.

Grilled Tuna

with Warm Bean Salad

Serves 4

1¼ cups dried white beans
5 tablespoons extra virgin olive oil,
    plus extra for brushing
1 tablespoon lemon juice
1 clove garlic, finely chopped
Salt and freshly ground black pepper
1 small red onion, very finely sliced
1 tablespoon chopped fresh parsley
4 tuna steaks, about 6 ounces each
Fresh parsley sprigs, to garnish
Lemon wedges, to serve

1 Cover the beans in at least twice the volume of cold water and let soak for 8 hours or overnight.

2 When you're ready to cook, drain and rinse the beans and place in a saucepan with twice their volume of fresh water. Bring slowly to a boil, skimming off any scum that rises to the surface. Boil the beans hard for 10 minutes, then reduce the heat and simmer for a further 1¼ -1½ hours, or until tender.

3 Meanwhile, mix the olive oil, lemon juice, garlic, and salt and pepper together in a bowl. Drain the beans thoroughly and mix together with the olive oil mixture, onion, and parsley. Taste for seasoning and set aside.

4 Preheat a ridged stovetop grill pan. Wash and dry the tuna steaks. Brush lightly with oil and season. Cook on the preheated grill pan for 2 minutes on each side until just pink in the center. Divide the bean salad among 4 serving plates. Top each with a tuna steak. Garnish each one with parsley sprigs and serve with lemon wedges.

Menu

Grilled Tuna with
Warm Bean Salad
~
Zucchini Bread
(p.208)
~
Stove-top
Rice Pudding with
Dried Fruit
(p.245)

Baked Fish
with Celeriac

Serves 4

1 tablespoon olive oil
1 large onion, finely chopped
Salt and freshly ground black pepper
1 celeriac, peeled and cut into short,
    fine strips (julienne)
2¼ pounds thick white fish fillet, in
    4 portions
2 tablespoons chopped fresh parsley
1 cup grated mature cheddar cheese

Menu

*Baked Fish
with Celeriac*

~

*Roasted Vegetables
with Pine Nuts
& Parmesan
(p.187)*

~

*Tropical Fruit Salad
(p.221)*

1 Preheat the oven to 400°F. Heat the oil in a saucepan. Add the onion with salt and pepper, stir well, then cover and cook gently for 10 minutes. Add the celeriac, stir well and cook for a further 10 minutes, stirring occasionally.

2 Turn the celeriac and onion mixture into a shallow, ovenproof dish. Arrange the portions of fish on top and season well. Sprinkle with the parsley, then with the cheese. Cook in the oven for about 20 minutes, or until the cheese is bubbling and golden brown and the fish is just cooked. Serve at once.

Fish Stick Sandwiches

with Mayonnaise

Serves 2

8 fish sticks
Butter, for spreading
4 slices white bread
A little mayonnaise
A little tomato ketchup
Salt and freshly ground black pepper

Menu

*Fish Stick
Sandwiches with
Mayonnaise*

~

*Caesar Salad
(p.194)*

~

*Peanut Butter
Brownies
(p.240)*

Tip

Simple and super quick, this sandwich is an absolute winner for a children's party when something savory is needed to balance out the sweets.

1 Cook the fish sticks according to the instructions on the package. Butter the slices of bread and spread two of them with a little mayonnaise and ketchup.

2 Put the cooked fish sticks on top of the mayonnaise and ketchup, and season with a little salt and pepper. Put the remaining slices of bread on top and serve at once.

Roast Cod with Fried Gremolata Bread Crumbs

Serves 4

2 cloves garlic, peeled
1 large bunch of fresh parsley
4 teaspoons grated lemon zest
2 cups bread crumbs, made from
   stale ciabatta
2 tablespoons olive oil, plus extra
   for oiling
4 thick skinless cod fillets, about
   7 ounces each
1½ teaspoons Dijon mustard

Menu

*Roast Cod with
Fried Gremolata
Bread Crumbs*

~

*Eggplant
Parmigiana
(p.144)*

Tip

Gremolata is a flavoring
which originates from Milan,
made of finely chopped lemon
zest, garlic, and parsley. It is
usually added after a dish
is cooked.

1 Preheat the oven to 400°F. Put the garlic and parsley on a board and finely chop with a mezzaluna or sharp knife. Put in a bowl and stir in the lemon zest, bread crumbs, and oil.

2 Toast in a skillet for 4-5 minutes, or until crisp and golden.

3 Put the cod fillets on an oiled baking sheet. Lightly brush with the Dijon mustard and pat the bread crumbs over the top of the fish. Cook in the oven for 10-12 minutes, or until the fish feels firm to the touch.

New England Fishballs

Makes about 25

2 tablespoons oil, plus extra for frying
1 onion, finely chopped
1¼ pounds cod fillet, roughly chopped
1 tablespoon chopped fresh tarragon
1 tablespoon chopped fresh parsley
Grated zest of 1 lemon
¼ cup heavy cream
1 egg

Menu

New England Fishballs

~

Stir-fried Brown Rice & Vegetables (p.202)

~

Chocolate Fondue with Marshmallows (p.230)

1 Heat the oil in a skillet over a medium heat. Add the onion and cook for 10 minutes until softened and just golden. Set aside until cold.

2 Put the onion, cod, and the remaining ingredients in a food processor and pulse until well mixed.

3 Shape the fish mixture into walnut-sized balls and chill for 30 minutes.

4 Heat a little oil in a skillet and cook the fishballs for 3-4 minutes each side until golden.

Smoked Trout Terrine

with Cucumber Salad

Serves 6

1½ tablespoons butter

2 tablespoons all-purpose flour

1¼ cups milk

1 tablespoon fresh grated horseradish
  or good quality horseradish sauce

Salt and freshly ground black pepper

1½ cup mayonnaise

4 smoked trout fillets, about 3-ounces
  each, skinned

Juice of 1 lemon

5–6 tablespoons cold water

4 sheets gelatin or 1 tablespoon
  granulated gelatin

2 egg whites

For the cucumber salad

1 cucumber, very thinly sliced

2 tablespoons white wine vinegar

1 tablespoon snipped fresh dill

Menu

Smoked Trout
Terrine with
Cucumber Salad
~
New England
Potato Salad
(p.172)
~
Double-crust
Apple Pie
(p.228)

1 Melt the butter in a saucepan, stir in the flour and cook for 2-3 minutes. Slowly add the milk, beating to form a smooth, thick sauce. Add the horseradish and season. Let cool for 15 minutes, then stir in the mayonnaise. Flake the trout into the mayonnaise mixture.

2 Mix the lemon juice with the cold water in a small saucepan and soak the gelatin for 5 minutes. Heat the gelatin until it has dissolved. Pour into the mousse mixture and mix.

3 Whisk the egg whites in a clean bowl until soft peaks form and fold into the smoked trout mixture. Spoon into a 3-quart terrine, which has been lined with plastic wrap. Cover and chill for 3-4 hours.

4 For the cucumber salad, place the cucumber in a shallow bowl. Pour the white wine vinegar over and stir in the dill. Season with black pepper.

5 To serve, invert the terrine onto a plate and serve in slices, along with the cucumber salad.

Harissa-coated Monkfish

Serves 4

2¹⁄₃ cups couscous
1¹⁄₂ cups boiling water
2 scallions, finely chopped
1 small bunch of fresh cilantro, finely
   chopped
6 ready-to-eat dried apricots, roughly
   chopped
¹⁄₃ cup almonds, toasted and roughly
   chopped
¹⁄₂ cup raisins
1 tablespoon lemon juice
¹⁄₄ cup olive oil
Salt and freshly ground black pepper
1¹⁄₄ pounds monkfish tails

For the harissa
4 dried chiles
2 fresh red chiles
2 cloves garlic
2 teaspoons cumin seeds
2 teaspoons coriander seeds
2 teaspoons caraway seeds
1 tablespoon fresh lemon juice
3 tablespoons olive oil

1 Preheat the oven to 400°F. For the harissa, soak the dried chiles in boiling water for 30 minutes.

Put the fresh chiles in an oven dish and roast for 20 minutes.

2 Remove the stalks from the dried and fresh chiles and put, whole, in a food processor. Add the remaining harissa ingredients and process until smooth. Spoon into a jar and chill until needed.

3 Put the couscous in a bowl and pour over the boiling water. Cover with plastic wrap and let stand for 15 minutes, then fluff up with a fork.

4 Stir in the remaining ingredients, except 1 tablespoon oil and the monkfish tails, into the couscous. Season and transfer to a serving dish.

5 Cut the fish into 2-inch medallions and put in a mixing bowl. Stir in 4 teaspoons of harissa and mix to coat every piece with the paste. Heat the remaining oil in a large skillet and fry the fish for 2–3 minutes on each side. Arrange on top of the couscous and pour any pan juices over the top.

Menu

*Harissa-coated
Monkfish*
~
*Stir-fried Greens
with Shiitake
Mushrooms
(p.179)*
~
*Caramel Ice Cream
(p.217)*

VEGETARIAN

- Roasted Beet Salad with Oranges & Goat Cheese
- Cheese & Tomato Pizza
- Chakchouka
- Cheese Fondue
- Cheese Soufflé
- Baked Macaroni & Cheese
- Eggs Benedict
- Parsley & Leek Frittata
- Spanish Omelet
- Onion Quiche
- Pasta with Fresh Tomato Sauce
- Baked Spinach Gnocchi
- Risotto Primavera
- Roast Vegetable Lasagne

- Eggplant Parmigiana
- Tomato Risotto
- Pumpkin Couscous
- Vegetable Stir-fry
- Mixed Vegetable Curry
- Chili with Guacamole
- Spinach with Paneer
- Chow Mein with Snow Peas
- Roast Peppers with Mozzarella
- Provençal Ratatouille
- Potato Pancakes with Creamy Mushrooms
- Spinach Roulade
- Butternut Squash with Goat Cheese

CHAPTER FOUR

VEGETARIAN

Roasted Beet Salad
with Oranges & Goat Cheese

Serves 4

6 medium-sized fresh beets, scrubbed
1 tablespoon balsamic vinegar
1 teaspoon honey
4 tablespoons olive oil
2 oranges
5 ounces goat cheese
1 tablespoon snipped fresh chives

Menu

Roasted Beet Salad
with Oranges & Goat
Cheese
~
Grilled Corn with
Flavored Butter
(p.174)
~
New England
Blueberry Pancakes
(p.226)

Tip
As well as the lovely rich color it gives to soups, beet juice can be used to color homemade pasta.

1 Preheat the oven to 350°F. Pierce the beets with a skewer or point of a knife and put in a roasting pan. Roast for 1½ hours until tender. Cool, then peel off the skins. Cut into ½-inch thick slices and put into a serving bowl.

2 Mix the vinegar, honey, and oil together and pour over the roasted beets.

3 With a serrated fruit knife, peel the oranges and cut into segments. Add to the beets and crumble the goat cheese on top. Scatter with chives before serving.

Cheese & Tomato Pizza

Serves 4

3½ cups strong bread flour, plus extra
    for dusting
1 teaspoon salt
1 teaspoon dried mixed herbs
1 tablespoon rapid-rise dried yeast
1–1¼ cups hand hot water
Vegetable oil, for oiling

For the topping
Two 14-ounce cans chopped tomatoes
4 tablespoons tomato paste
2 cloves garlic, crushed
2 teaspoons sugar
4 ounces cheese, such as cheddar or
    Emmental, grated
6 olives

1 Put the flour in a bowl, add the salt, herbs, and yeast. Stir well. Add enough warm water to form a smooth dough. Turn on to a floured surface and knead for 10 minutes.

2 Put the dough in a large bowl that has been lightly brushed with oil. Leave in a warm place for about 1 hour, or until the dough has doubled in size.

3 For the topping, put the chopped tomatoes, tomato paste, garlic, and sugar in a large skillet and bring the mixture to a boil. Reduce the heat and simmer for 40 minutes until thickened.

4 Roll out the dough into a 13 x 10-inch rectangle, and put on an oiled baking sheet. Spread the tomato sauce over the dough, leaving a 1-inch gap around the edge. Sprinkle over the cheese and olives, and leave to rise in a warm place for 10 minutes. Preheat the oven to 425°F. Bake for 20 minutes. Cut into squares and serve warm.

Menu

Cheese & Tomato Pizza

~

Green Bean & Mozzarella Salad (p.201)

~

Roasted Corn Salsa (p.162)

Chakchouka

Spicy Baked Peppers

Serves 4

4 tablespoons olive oil

2 large onions, finely chopped

2 red bell peppers, seeded and cut into
1-inch pieces

1 yellow bell pepper, seeded and cut
into 1-inch pieces pieces

1 green bell pepper, seeded and cut
into 1-inch pieces

8 large vine-ripened tomatoes, peeled,
seeded, and chopped

3 cloves garlic, peeled

1 small fresh green chile

1 teaspoon paprika

1 teaspoon ground cumin

2 teaspoons salt

1 teaspoon freshly ground
black pepper

4 eggs

1 tablespoon finely chopped fresh
parsley or cilantro, to garnish

Steamed couscous, to serve

Menu

Chakchouka

~

Chocolate Mousse
(p.232)

1 Preheat the oven to 350°F. Heat 2 tablespoons of the oil in a heavy-based skillet. Add the onions and peppers and sauté over high heat until the onions are soft but not brown. Add the tomatoes and simmer, uncovered, for 20–30 minutes, or until all the liquid has evaporated.

2 Using a mortar and pestle or a food processor, purée the garlic with the chile, paprika, cumin, and salt and pepper. Stir the paste into the cooked vegetables.

3 Transfer the mixture to an ovenproof dish. Smooth the surface, then make four depressions with the back of a spoon. Break an egg into each depression and sprinkle the remaining oil evenly over the top of the eggs and vegetables. Cook in the oven for 10 minutes, or until the eggs are just set. Sprinkle with parsley or cilantro and serve with steaming couscous.

Cheese Fondue

Serves 4–6

Menu

Cheese Fondue

~

Roasted Vegetables with Pine Nuts & Parmesan (p.187)

3 cloves garlic, bruised
2½ cups dry white wine
6 cups grated Gruyère or Emmental cheese
3 tablespoons arrowroot or flour
⅓ stick (3 tablespoons) butter
Salt and freshly ground white pepper
Freshly grated nutmeg
¼ cup whipping cream
3 tablespoons Kirsch
French bread, cut into cubes and lightly toasted, to serve
Boiled small new potatoes, to serve

1 Bring the garlic and white wine to a boil in a medium, heavy-based saucepan. Boil until reduced by about a quarter. Remove and discard the garlic and reduce the heat to low.

2 Toss the cheese with the arrowroot or flour in a bowl. Add half the butter to the wine and begin adding the cheese a little at a time, stirring with a wooden fork or spoon until each addition has completely melted before adding more. When all the cheese has been added, season with salt, pepper, and freshly grated nutmeg to taste.

3 Add the remaining butter and half the cream and continue to cook for 2–3 minutes, until the mixture thickens to resemble thick custard in texture. Add the remaining cream and then stir in the Kirsch.

4 Pour the fondue into a warm fondue pot and set over its burner. Serve with the bread and vegetables. Provide long-handled fondue forks to spear and dunk pieces of bread or vegetable into the fondue. Using a twisting motion to remove the food from the fondue catches the delicious drips.

Cheese Soufflé

Serves 4

$^1/_3$ stick (3 tablespoons) butter, plus
    extra for greasing
2 tablespoons grated fresh
    Parmesan cheese,
$^1/_2$ cup all-purpose flour
1$^1/_4$ cups milk
4 eggs, separated
$^3/_4$ cup grated Gruyère, Emmental
    or Appenzeller
2 tablespoons fresh chives, snipped
Salt and freshly ground black pepper

1 Preheat the oven to 375°F. Set the shelves in the oven so that the top shelf is in the center of the oven with no shelves or grill pan above it. Generously grease a 3-quart soufflé dish. Sprinkle the Parmesan cheese into the dish and turn it so that the cheese sticks to the butter on the sides and bottom. Set aside.

2 Melt the butter in a medium saucepan. Add the flour and stir well until smooth. Cook gently for 1–2 minutes, then remove the pan from the heat and add about 3 tablespoons of the milk. Stir well using a wooden spoon. The mixture will appear lumpy and dry but keep stirring until smooth. Add another 3 tablespoons of the milk and stir again.

Keep adding milk gradually and stirring until smooth. When half the milk is added, switch to a whisk and continue adding the milk in small amounts.

3 When all the milk is added, return the pan to medium heat. Bring slowly up to a boil, whisking continuously, until thickened and bubbling. Reduce the heat to a gentle simmer and cook for 2 minutes, then remove. Cover and let cool for 5–10 minutes.

4 Add the egg yolks and whisk in thoroughly. Add the cheese and chives and stir together. Season generously—the egg white is going to dilute this mixture, so it's fine to overseason.

5 Put the egg whites into a very clean bowl and whisk until stiff peaks form. Transfer a large spoonful of egg white to the cheese mixture and fold together. Add the remaining egg white and fold together carefully, but thoroughly. Pour the mixture into the soufflé dish and transfer to the center shelf of the oven. Bake for 25–30 minutes until well risen but firm. It should be soft, not liquid, in the middle.

Menu

Cheese Soufflé
~
Caesar Salad
(p.194)
~
Maple-baked Acorn
Squash (p.189)

Baked Macaroni & Cheese

Serves 4–6

½ stick (4 tablespoons) butter, plus
   extra for dotting
Salt and freshly ground black
   pepper
1 pound macaroni
1 large onion, finely chopped
½ cup all-purpose flour
4 cups milk
1 bay leaf
½ teaspoon chopped fresh thyme, plus
   extra to garnish
½ teaspoon cayenne pepper
1 teaspoon mustard powder
2 small leeks, finely chopped,
   blanched, and drained
3¾ cups grated mature cheddar cheese
2 tablespoons plain dry bread crumbs
2 tablespoons freshly grated
   Parmesan cheese

1 Preheat the oven to 350°F and lightly grease a 13 x 9-inch baking dish. Cook the macaroni in a large saucepan of boiling water for about 10 minutes, or until al dente. Drain and rinse under cold running water, then set aside.

2 Melt the butter in a heavy-based saucepan, over medium-low heat. Add the onion and cook until translucent, stirring frequently. Sprinkle over the flour and stir until blended. Cook for 2–3 minutes.

Menu

*Baked Macaroni
& Cheese*
~
*Waldorf Salad
(p.196)*
~
*Chocolate Mousse
(p.232)*

3 Whisk in 1 cup of the milk, then gradually whisk in the remaining 3 cups. Add the bay leaf, thyme, season with salt, and then simmer for about 15 minutes, or until thick and smooth. Season with the black pepper, cayenne, and mustard powder.

4 Remove the sauce from the heat and stir in the drained leeks and all but a handful of the grated cheddar. When the cheese has melted and is well blended, stir in the cooked macaroni. Transfer to the baking dish and spread out evenly. Put the dish on a large baking sheets.

5 Sprinkle the remaining cheddar over the macaroni. Combine the bread crumbs and Parmesan, and sprinkle on top. Dot with butter and cook in the oven for 30 minutes, or until well browned and crisp. Garnish with thyme and serve.

Eggs Benedict

Serves 4

1 tablespoon white wine vinegar
4 extra large, very fresh eggs
2 English muffins, split, toasted, and
buttered
Watercress sprigs, to garnish

For the Hollandaise Sauce
3 egg yolks
2 tablespoons freshly squeezed lemon
juice
$^1/_2$ teaspoon salt
Pinch of cayenne pepper
1 stick (8 tablespoons) butter
2 tablespoons light cream

1 Prepare the Hollandaise sauce first. Put the egg yolks and lemon juice in a blender or food processor. Season with salt and cayenne pepper to taste and process for 15 seconds until blended.

2 Melt the butter in a small saucepan over a medium heat until bubbling and skim off any foam. With the motor running, pour the hot butter into the blender or food processor in a thin, steady stream—do not pour in the milky solids at the bottom of the pan.

3 Process for a few seconds until the sauce is well blended. Add the cream and pulse until blended. Scrape the sauce into a heatproof bowl and keep warm over hot water.

4 Bring about 1-inch depth of water to a boil in a large skillet. Stir in the vinegar. Break an egg into a cup. Using a wooden spoon, stir the water in a corner of the pan to create a swirl or vortex, then gently slide the egg into the middle. Repeat with the remaining eggs.

5 Reduce the heat and simmer for 3–4 minutes until the eggs are lightly cooked or set to your taste. Using a slotted spoon, transfer the eggs to a plate lined with paper towels to drain. Trim off any ragged edges of egg white.

6 Top each buttered muffin half with a poached egg. Spoon a little warm sauce over the eggs, garnish each with a sprig of watercress and serve.

Menu

Eggs Benedict
~
Green Bean &
Mozzarella Salad
(p.201)
~
Chilled Tangerine
& Lemon Mousse
(p.233)

Parsley & Leek Frittata

Serves 4

3 leeks
¼ stick (2 tablespoons) butter
2 small bunches of fresh parsley
4 large eggs
Salt and freshly ground black pepper

Menu

Parsley & Leek Frittata

~

Grapefruit, Shrimp & Avocado Salad (p.102)

Tip
Various fillings may be used such as diced mushrooms, asparagus, spinach, or cooked diced potato.

1 Finely slice the leeks on the diagonal. Melt the butter in a medium-sized ovenproof skillet and add the leeks. Cook for 8–10 minutes until soft.

2 Preheat the broiler. Remove the stalks from the parsley and finely chop with a mezzaluna. Stir into the leeks.

3 Beat the eggs and season with salt and pepper. Pour into the skillet and cook gently for about 10 minutes. The base of the frittata should be set, but the top will be wobbly.

4 Place the skillet under the broiler and cook for 3–4 minutes until the top is set and golden.

Spanish Omelet

Serves 2

2 potatoes, peeled and thinly sliced
¼ cup olive oil
1 large onion, thinly sliced
2 eggs
Salt and freshly ground black pepper
Crusty bread, to serve

Menu

Spanish Omelet

~

Panzanella
(p.198)

~

Spiced Baked Apples
(p.224)

1 Heat the oil in a skillet. Add the potato and onion and cook very gently until tender, without browning if possible.

2 While the potato and onion are cooking, beat the eggs with some seasoning in a large bowl.

3 Lift the potato and onion from the pan using a slotted spoon and add to the eggs. Drain all but about 1 tablespoon of the oil from the pan. Return the egg mixture to the pan, shaking it to distribute everything evenly. Cook gently until the egg is set and lightly golden on the bottom.

4 Put a plate that is larger than the pan over the top and carefully invert the omelet on to it. Slide the omelet back into the pan, cooked-side-uppermost, and continue to cook until the bottom is set and golden. This omelet can be served hot, warm, or cold.

Onion Quiche

Serves 6

1 stick (8 tablespoons) butter
1²/₃ flour, plus extra for dusting
2 tablespoons cold water

For the filling
¹/₄ stick (2 tablespoons) butter
1 pound onions, thinly sliced
3 eggs, beaten
1¹/₄ cups light cream
3 tablespoons dry sherry
Pinch of ground mace
Salt and freshly ground black pepper

1 To make the dough, rub the butter into the flour until the mixture resembles fine bread crumbs. Stir in the cold water to form a dough, then knead lightly. Wrap in plastic wrap and chill for 30 minutes.

2 Roll out the dough on a lightly floured surface and use to line a 10-inch loose-bottom tart pan or quiche dish. Prick the base all over and chill for a further 30 minutes.

3 Preheat the oven to 400°F. Line the pastry shell with parchment paper and weigh down with baking beans or dried beans.

Bake for 10 minutes, then remove the beans and paper. Reduce the oven temperature to 350°F.

4 Meanwhile, make the filling. Melt the butter in a heavy-based saucepan and add the onions. Stir well, then cook for 10 minutes, or until softened but not browned. Remove from the heat and let cool slightly.

5 Beat the eggs with the cream, sherry, mace and plenty of seasoning. Use a slotted spoon to transfer the cooked onions to the pastry shell, distributing them evenly over the base, and pour any cooking juices into the egg mixture. Stir well, then pour the mixture over the onions. Bake the quiche for about 45 minutes, or until the filling is set and golden brown. Let cool for 15 minutes before serving. The quiche can be enjoyed warm or cold.

Menu

Onion Quiche
~
Roasted Vegetables with Pine Nuts & Parmesan (p.187)
~
Meringues with Cream & Blueberries (p.223)

Pasta with Fresh Tomato Sauce

Serves 2

2¼ pounds ripe plum or beef tomatoes
3 tablespoons olive oil
1 small onion, finely chopped
1 clove garlic, crushed
2 tablespoons chopped fresh basil
Pinch of sugar
Salt and freshly ground black pepper
4 ounces dried pasta of your choice
Freshly grated Parmesan cheese,
   to serve
Green salad, to serve

1 Put the tomatoes into a large bowl and pour boiling water over to cover. Leave for 30 seconds, then drain and refresh under cold water. Using a sharp knife, prick the skin of each tomato - it should split and come away easily from the tomato. If not, you may have to repeat the process for a further 30 seconds. Skin the tomatoes and chop. Set aside.

2 Heat the oil in a large saucepan. Add the onion and cook over medium heat for about 5 minutes, stirring frequently, until softened but not browned. Add the garlic and cook for a further 30 seconds. Add the tomatoes, basil, and sugar and stir well. Bring to a boil and cover. Simmer for 30 minutes. Remove the lid and simmer, uncovered, for 30-45 minutes until thickened. Taste and adjust the seasoning.

3 Cook the pasta according to the instructions on the packet and serve immediately with the fresh tomato sauce, sprinkled with Parmesan cheese, and a green salad on the side. Alternatively, this sauce can be frozen for up to 3 months.

Menu

Pasta with Fresh Tomato Sauce
~
Old-fashioned Cornbread (p.210)

Baked Spinach Gnocchi

Serves 4

3 tablespoons extra virgin olive oil
2 scallions, chopped
1 clove garlic, crushed
8 ounces fresh spinach leaves
2 cups milk
³/₄ cup semolina
Freshly grated nutmeg
1 egg, beaten
³/₄ cup freshly grated Parmesan cheese
Salt and freshly ground black pepper

1 Heat the olive oil, scallons, and garlic in a large saucepan. When the onions begin to sizzle, add the spinach and stir well. Cover and cook for 30 seconds. Stir, then remove from the heat.

2 Cool the spinach slightly, then transfer the mixture to a blender and finely chop. If you do not have a blender, drain bundles of the mixture, reserving all the liquid, and chop them by hand, then return them to the reserved juices.

3 Pour the milk into the pan used to cook the spinach and heat until boiling. Sprinkle in the semolina, stirring all the time. Cook until boiling, first stirring, then beating as it thickens. After 1 minute, the semolina should be thick and come away from the sides of the pan. Remove from the heat and stir in the spinach mixture. Season and add nutmeg to taste. Let cool slightly, then beat in the egg.

4 Lightly oil a shallow dish. Turn the semolina mixture out onto it, spreading the mixture to a rectangle of about 7 x 10 inches. Pat the edges with a knife, cover with plastic wrap, and chill for at least 2 hours.

5 Preheat the oven to 400°F and lightly oil a 10-inch round ovenproof dish. Cut the semolina into 3 strips slightly more than 2 inches wide. Wet the knife, then wipe with paper towels; wet it again between cuts. Cut the mixture at 10-inch intervals in the opposite direction to give 15 gnocchi.

6 Dip each square in grated Parmesan to coat both sides, and place in the dish. Overlap the squares around the edge of the dish, then place a few in the middle to fill. Sprinkle with remaining Parmesan and bake in the oven for 30 minutes until crisp and golden on top. Serve immediately.

Menu

Baked Spinach Gnocchi
~
Hot Vegetable Salad
(p.184)
~
Apple Cake Bars
(p.241)

Risotto Primavera

Serves 6

¹/₄ stick (2 tablespoons) butter
1 tablespoon olive oil
1 onion, finely chopped
1 rib celery, finely chopped
2 carrots, peeled and finely chopped
1³/₄ cups arborio rice
3 cups vegetable broth
¹/₂ cup freshly shelled peas
2 medium zucchini, finely chopped
Salt and freshly ground black pepper
Small bunch of fresh mint, finely
  chopped
Small bunch of fresh parsley, finely
  chopped
Shavings of Parmesan cheese, to serve

Menu

Risotto Primavera

~

Caesar Salad
(p.194)

~

Summer Berry
Shortcakes
(p.246)

1 Melt the butter with the oil in a large heavy-based saucepan and add the vegetables. Cover and cook for 15 minutes.

2 Add the rice to the pan and stir well to coat the grains of rice. Pour in ½ cup broth and stir. Cook until the liquid has been absorbed.

3 Add another ½ cup of broth and the peas, stir a few times and again let the rice absorb the liquid. Continue in this way for 25 minutes leaving ½ cup of broth aside.

4 Stir the zucchini into the risotto with the remaining broth. Stir well and season with salt and pepper.

5 Mix the fresh herbs into the risotto and serve immediately with Parmesan shavings.

Roast Vegetable Lasagne

Serves 4

1 large red bell pepper, seeded and cut
   into chunks
2 small zucchini, cut into chunks
2 red onions, each cut into 8 wedges
4 cloves garlic
1 medium eggplant, cut into chunks
2 tablespoons olive oil
2 large fresh thyme sprigs
2 fresh bay leaves
Two 16-ounce jars fresh tomato sauce
9-ounce jar artichokes in oil, drained
   and halved if large
$\frac{1}{2}$ cup sun-dried tomatoes
4 tablespoons freshly grated Parmesan
1 pound ricotta cheese
2 eggs, beaten
Salt and freshly ground black pepper
About 9 fresh lasagne sheets

1 Preheat the oven to 400°F. Toss the pepper, zucchini, onions, garlic cloves, and eggplant with the oil in a large bowl. Tip everything onto a shallow roasting pan or heavy-based baking sheet. Tuck the thyme sprigs and bay leaves among the vegetables. Cook near the top of the oven, turning twice, for about 40 minutes until tender and golden at the edges. Reduce the oven temperature to 375°F.

2 Remove the whole herbs. Mix the vegetables with the tomato sauce, artichokes, and sun-dried tomatoes. Set aside.

3 Reserve about 3 tablespoons of the Parmesan cheese, then, in a large bowl, beat the ricotta until soft, then mix in the eggs, remaining Parmesan cheese, and plenty of seasoning. Set aside.

4 Spread a large spoonful of the vegetable mixture over the bottom of an ovenproof dish measuring about 8 x 10 x 2½ inches. Trimming the sheets to fit, top with a layer of pasta. Now add half the remaining vegetable mixture and top with half the remaining pasta. Add the last of the vegetable mixture and the final layer of pasta and top with the ricotta mixture. Sprinkle with the reserved Parmesan cheese.

5 Bake in the center of the oven for about 40–45 minutes, or until bubbling and golden.

Menu

Roast Vegetable Lasagne
~
*Panzanella
(p.198)*
~
*Caramel Ice Cream
(p.217)*

Eggplant Parmigiana

Serves 6

Olive oil, for oiling and frying
2 eggs, beaten with 1 tablespoon water
$^2/_3$ cup plain dry bread crumbs
1 large eggplant, cut into ½-inch slices
$^1/_3$ cup freshly grated Parmesan cheese
8 ounces mozzarella cheese, thinly sliced

For the tomato sauce
2 tablespoons olive oil
1 large onion, finely chopped
2–3 cloves garlic, finely chopped
Two 14-ounce cans chopped tomatoes
2 teaspoons brown sugar
1 bay leaf
1 teaspoon dried oregano
1 teaspoon dried basil
Salt and freshly ground black pepper
2 tablespoons shredded fresh basil

1 For the tomato sauce, heat the oil in a heavy-based saucepan. Cook the onion for 7 minutes, or until it is soft and translucent, stirring occasionally. Add the garlic and cook for another minute, then add the tomatoes, sugar, bay leaf, oregano, and dried basil, and bring to a boil, stirring frequently. Reduce the heat and simmer, stirring occasionally, for 30-45 minutes, or until the sauce has thickened. Season, stir in the basil and remove from the heat.

2 Lightly oil a large, shallow baking dish and set aside. Put the beaten egg in a shallow dish and the bread crumbs on a sheet of waxed paper. Dip slices of eggplant into the egg mixture and then into the bread crumbs to coat each side completely.

3 Heat 2–3 tablespoons oil in a heavy-based skillet. Cook a few eggplant slices at a time, turning regularly, until golden. Add more oil if needed. Drain on paper towels. Repeat with all the slices.

4 Preheat the oven to 350°F. Spread a little tomato sauce in the dish. Arrange a layer of eggplant slices over the sauce, sprinkle with Parmesan and top with a layer of mozzarella slices, then cover with a layer of sauce. Repeat the layers, ending with a thin layer of tomato sauce and a sprinkle of Parmesan. Drizzle a little oil on top and bake for 35 minutes, or until bubbling and brown.

Menu

Eggplant
Parmigiana
~
Texas Pilaf
(p.203)

Tomato Risotto

Serves 4

1 pound tomatoes, skinned and halved
$\frac{1}{4}$ cup extra virgin olive oil
1 large onion, finely chopped
1 clove garlic, crushed
1$\frac{1}{3}$ cups arborio or risotto rice
1 cup dry white wine
2$\frac{1}{2}$ cups vegetable broth
Salt and freshly ground black pepper
1 teaspoon sugar

Menu

Tomato Risotto
~
Braised Fennel
(p.177)
~
Mango Ice Cream
(p.216)

1 Scoop the seeds and any soft pulp out of the tomatoes into a sieve. Press the pulp through the sieve and discard the seeds. Finely dice the tomato shells and set both these and the sieved pulp aside.

2 Heat the olive oil in a large saucepan. Add the onion and garlic and cook, stirring occasionally, for about 5 minutes, or until the onion has softened slightly. Add the rice and stir until all the grains are coated in oil. Pour in the wine and the sieved tomato pulp, then bring to a boil. Reduce the heat and simmer, uncovered, stirring once or twice, until the liquid is virtually absorbed.

3 Meanwhile, heat the broth to simmering point in a separate saucepan. Keeping it just below simmering point, add about a quarter of the broth to the risotto with seasoning to taste. Stir well and simmer until all the broth has been absorbed. Add the remaining broth in 3 batches, simmering until each batch is absorbed before adding the next. Stir in the diced tomatoes and sugar with the final batch of broth.

4 Remove the risotto from the heat and cover the pan tightly, then let stand for 5 minutes. Fork up the rice and season, then serve at once.

Pumpkin Couscous

Serves 4

3 tablespoons olive oil

2 cloves garlic, crushed

2 onions, finely chopped

1 green bell pepper, seeded and chopped

1 yellow bell pepper, seeded and chopped

1 tablespoon dried sage

2 pounds cooked pumpkin cut into
 $^1/_2$-inch cubes

Two 14-ounce cans chopped tomatoes

14-ounce can chickpeas, drained

Salt and freshly ground black pepper

2 cups couscous

$1^2/_3$ cups boiling water

1 large mild green chile, such as
 Anaheim, seeded and chopped

1 hot chile, such as jalapeño or
 serrano, seeded and chopped

Grated zest of 1 lemon

3 tablespoons chopped fresh parsley,
 plus extra to garnish

A little extra virgin olive oil (optional)

1 Heat the olive oil in a saucepan. Add the garlic, onions, and green and yellow peppers. Stir well, then cover the pan and cook over a medium heat for 15 minutes until the vegetables have softened.

2 Stir in the sage and pumpkin, then pour in the tomatoes with their juice. Mix in the chickpeas and season with salt and pepper. Bring to a boil, reduce the heat and cover. Simmer for 25–30 minutes.

3 When the pumpkin has been cooking for 5-10 minutes, place the couscous in a heatproof bowl. Sprinkle with a little salt. Pour in the boiling water, cover and let stand for 15 minutes. In a separate bowl, mix the mild and hot chiles with the lemon zest and parsley.

4 Taste the pumpkin and season if necessary. Add the chile, lemon, and parsley mixture and remove from the heat. Stir lightly. Fluff the couscous with a fork and drizzle with a little extra virgin olive oil, if using, then season with freshly ground black pepper. Divide the couscous among 4 large warm bowls. Ladle the pumpkin casserole over the couscous, garnish with parsley, and serve at once.

Menu

Pumpkin
Couscous

~

Green Bean &
Mozzarella Salad
(p.201)

~

Old-fashioned
Cornbread (p.210)

Vegetable Stir-fry

Serves 4

Menu

Vegetable Stir-fry
~
Coconut Rice
(p.206)

12 ounces mixed prepared vegetables,
   such as baby corn, red pepper, bok
   choy, mushrooms, broccoli, carrot
2 tablespoons light soy sauce
1 tablespoon rice wine or dry sherry
2 tablespoons vegetable broth or water
2 tablespoons peanut oil
12 ounces cubed tofu
2 cloves garlic, finely chopped
1-inch piece fresh ginger, chopped
3 scallions, finely chopped
1 red chile, seeded and finely chopped
1 teaspoon cornstarch
1 teaspoon water
1 teaspoon sesame oil
Toasted cashews, shredded scallions
   and bean sprouts, to garnish

1 Halve the baby corn lengthwise, seed and thinly slice the red pepper, tear or shred the bok choy, slice the mushrooms, break the broccoli into florets and slice the carrot into batons. Mix the soy sauce, rice wine and broth together, then set aside.

2 Put the wok over a high heat until it is very hot. Add the peanut oil and swirl it to lightly coat the wok. Leave for a few seconds until the oil is almost smoking—a fine haze will appear.

3 Add the tofu and move it around the wok continuously for 1–2 minutes, or until it starts to brown.

4 Add the garlic, ginger, scallions and chile. Cook for a few seconds, continuing to stir.

5 Add the prepared vegetables in the following order: carrot, broccoli, pepper and mushrooms. Cook for about 1 minute before adding the baby corn and bok choy. Cook for another minute, still stirring and turning everything over a high heat.

6 Add the soy sauce mixture to the wok. Mix the cornstarch with the water until smooth. Add to the wok and stir. Bring to a boil, reduce the heat and simmer for 1 minute until thickened and everything is coated in sauce. Remove from the heat.

7 Add the sesame oil and mix together well. Transfer the stir-fry to serving bowls and scatter over the toasted cashews, shredded scallions, and bean sprouts.

Mixed Vegetable Curry

Serves 6

- ¾ stick (6 tablespoons) butter
- 1 large onion, finely chopped
- 2 cloves garlic, crushed
- 1-inch piece fresh ginger, finely chopped
- 1 teaspoon dark mustard seeds
- Seeds of 4 green cardamom pods
- 1 teaspoon ground cumin
- 1 teaspoon ground coriander
- 1 teaspoon ground turmeric
- 2 potatoes, cut into bite-sized pieces
- 2 carrots, cut into bite-sized sticks
- 2 green or red bell peppers, halved and cut into thick slices
- 4 ounces green beans, cut into thirds on the diagonal
- 2 eggplants, cut into 1-inch cubes
- 2 small zucchini, sliced
- 14-ounce can unsweetened coconut milk
- 1 teaspoon sugar
- 3 tablespoons chopped fresh cilantro
- 3 tablespoons chopped fresh mint
- 2 teaspoons salt
- 2 chopped fresh green chiles and/or 2 tablespoons unsweetened shredded coconut, to garnish

1 Heat the butter in a heavy-based saucepan or casserole. Add the onion, garlic, ginger, and mustard seeds and sauté over a high heat for 2 minutes. Add the cardamom seeds, cumin, ground coriander, and turmeric and cook for 1 minute.

2 Add the potatoes, coating well with the spice mixture. One at a time, add the carrots, peppers, green beans, eggplant, and zucchini, coating each with the spice mixture as before.

3 Add the coconut milk and sugar. Bring to a boil and add the coriander, mint, and salt. Reduce the heat and simmer for about 20 minutes, or until the vegetables are cooked. (Be careful not to overcook.)

4 Transfer to a serving dish and garnish with chiles and/or the coconut.

Menu

Mixed Vegetable Curry

~

Lychees with Orange & Ginger (p.229)

Chili with Guacamole

Serves 6

1¼ cups dried black beans
3 tablespoons olive oil
2 onions, chopped
2 cloves garlic, crushed
1 or 2 hot green chiles, seeded and
  finely chopped, to taste
2 tablespoons mild chili powder
1 teaspoon ground cumin
1 teaspoon paprika
Two 14-ounce cans chopped tomatoes
1 teaspoon dried oregano
Salt and freshly ground black pepper
Sour cream, to serve

For the guacamole

2 medium ripe avocados, peeled and
  finely chopped
1 small red onion, finely chopped
1 small red chile, seeded and finely
  chopped
2 small tomatoes, skinned, seeded, and
  diced
Juice of 1 lime
2 tablespoons fresh cilantro, chopped

1 Put the beans into a large bowl and cover with at least twice their volume of cold water. Let soak for 8 hours or overnight. Drain the beans and put into a large saucepan. Cover with fresh water and bring to a boil. Boil for 10 minutes, then reduce the heat and simmer for about 40 minutes until the beans are tender. Drain and set aside.

2 Heat the oil in a large saucepan. Add the onions and fry for 7–8 minutes until softened. Add the garlic and chiles and cook for 1 minute. Add the chili powder, cumin, and paprika and cook for 30 seconds before adding the tomatoes and oregano. Simmer gently, uncovered, for 20 minutes. Add the beans, stir well and simmer for a further 30–40 minutes until the chili has thickened. Season.

3 To make the guacamole, put the avocados into a non-reactive copper bowl. Add the onion, chilli, tomatoes, lime juice, and cilantro and mix well. Serve the chili in bowls with a spoonful of guacamole and sour cream on the side.

Menu

Chili with Guacamole
...
*Old-fashioned
Cornbread (p.210)*
...
*Tomato Salsa
(p.162)*

Spinach with Paneer

Serves 4

¼ stick (2 tablespoons) butter or ghee
8 ounces paneer, in one piece
1 large onion, chopped
1 clove garlic, crushed
1 tablespoon cumin seeds
1 teaspoon ground turmeric
Salt and freshly ground black pepper
2¼ pounds young spinach, coarsely
  shredded

Tip

If you can't find the Indian cheese called paneer, use medium tofu or the Mexican cheese *queso a freir.*

1 Melt the butter or ghee in a heavy-based saucepan. Add the paneer and cook until it is golden brown underneath, then use a spatula to turn it, and cook the other side. Remove from the pan, drain carefully and transfer to a plate.

2 Add the onion, garlic, and cumin seeds to the pan. Stir well, then cook over a medium heat for about 15 minutes until the onion has thoroughly softened and is beginning to brown in places. Stir frequently and keep the heat fairly low.

3 Stir in the turmeric with plenty of salt and pepper. Add the spinach to the pan and cover tightly. Cook for 2 minutes, or until the spinach has wilted. Meanwhile, cut the paneer into small cubes.

4 Stir the spinach with the onion and cooking juices. Taste and adjust the seasoning. Top with the paneer and cook for 2 minutes to heat the cheese slightly.

Menu

*Spinach
with Paneer*

~

*Emmental & Roasted
Corn Spoon Bread
(p.207)*

~

*Tropical
Fruit Salad
(p.221)*

Chow Mein
with Snow Peas

Serves 4

6 large dried shiitake mushrooms
12 ounces dried Chinese egg noodles
2 teaspoons cornstarch
6 tablespoons dry sherry
2 tablespoons light soy sauce
2 teaspoons sesame oil
2 tablespoons safflower oil
2 tablespoons chopped fresh
  ginger
2 cloves garlic, crushed
7 ounces snow peas, sliced
8 scallions, finely chopped

1 Put the mushrooms in a small bowl and pour in just enough boiling water to cover them. Leave to soak for 10 minutes, pressing the mushrooms into the water frequently so that they rehydrate. Drain and slice the mushrooms, reserving the soaking water and discarding any tough stems.

2 Put the dried egg noodles in a large bowl, breaking the sheets in half so that they fit easily and cover with plenty of boiling water. Cover and let soak for 10 minutes, or until tender. Blend the cornstarch to a smooth paste with the sherry, soy sauce, and sesame oil. Prepare a colander or sieve for draining the noodles before beginning to stir-fry the vegetables.

Menu

*Chow Mein
with Snow Peas*

~

*Stir-fried Greens
(p.179)*

~

*Lychees with
Orange & Ginger
(p.229)*

3 Heat the safflower oil in a wok or large skillet. Add the ginger and stir-fry for 30 seconds, then add the garlic, and stir-fry for another 30 seconds. Add the mushrooms and cook briefly, then add the snow peas and scallions. Stir-fry for 1 minute. Pour in the cornstarch mixture and bring to a boil, stirring until thickened.

4 Drain the noodles and add them to the vegetables. Toss all the ingredients together so they are thoroughly combined. Taste for seasoning and add more soy sauce if necessary. Serve immediately.

Roast Peppers
with Mozzarella

Serves 4

4 medium red bell peppers

16 ripe cherry tomatoes, skinned

4 fat cloves garlic, finely chopped

8 anchovy fillets, drained and finely chopped (optional)

Handful of fresh basil leaves, torn, plus extra, to garnish

8 tablespoons extra virgin olive oil

Freshly ground black pepper, to taste

5-ounce ball fresh mozzarella in water drained and chopped into 8 equal pieces

Crusty bread, to serve

Menu

Roast Peppers with Mozzarella

~

Broccoli Pilaf (p.205)

~

Chocolate-covered Doughnuts (p.238)

1 Preheat the oven to 400°F. Cut each pepper in half lengthwise through the stem. Scoop out the seeds and membranes. Put the pepper halves onto a large baking sheet.

2 Put two cherry tomatoes into each pepper half. Divide the garlic, anchovies (if using), and basil among the pepper halves. Drizzle each with 1 tablespoon of olive oil. Season with black pepper (the anchovies and cheese will add enough salt). Transfer the baking sheet to the oven and cook for 40 minutes until softened and starting to brown at the edges. Remove the sheet from the oven and divide the cheese among the peppers. Return to the oven for a further 10 minutes, or until the cheese is melted. Serve hot or warm with plenty of crusty bread.

Provençal Ratatouille

Serves 4

2 bulbs fennel, quartered lengthwise
3 red onions, quartered
6 cloves garlic, unpeeled
6 tablespoons olive oil
Salt and freshly ground black pepper
3 zucchini, chopped into $1/2$-inch slices
2 red bell peppers, seeded and cut into
  2-inch chunks
1 eggplant, cut into 2-inch chunks

For the tomato sauce
14-ounce can chopped tomatoes
$2/3$ cup white wine
2 tablespoons tomato paste
6 fresh thyme sprigs
1 teaspoon sugar

Menu

Provençal Ratatouille
~
Patatas Bravas
(p.167)
~
Applesauce Sundae
(p.236)

1 Preheat the oven to 400°F. Use 2 large roasting pans. Don't try to cram all the vegetables into one or they'll end up soggy and stewed instead of roasted. Blanch the fennel in boiling water for 5 minutes, then drain. Place the onions and fennel in a roasting pan with 3 unpeeled garlic cloves and half the oil. Season well with salt and pepper.

2 Put the zucchini, peppers, and eggplant into the second roasting pan. Pour the remaining oil over the vegetables and add the rest of the garlic cloves. Roast the fennel, onion, and garlic in the oven for 50 minutes, and the zucchini, peppers, eggplant, and garlic for 40 minutes.

3 Meanwhile, to make the tomato sauce, put the tomatoes in a saucepan and stir in the remaining ingredients. Simmer for 20 minutes until reduced and thickened. Remove the thyme sprigs and stir in the roasted vegetables.

Potato Pancakes

with Creamy Mushrooms

Serves 4 as a main course or 6 as a starter

Menu

Potato Pancakes with Creamy Mushrooms

~

Porgy with Garlic & Cilantro Butter (p.106)

~

Tropical Fruit Salad (p.221)

1 pound cooked floury potatoes
Salt and freshly ground black pepper
3 eggs, separated
¼ stick (2 tablespoons) butter
⅓ cup all-purpose flour
5 tablespoons milk
2 tablespoons olive oil, plus extra for frying
6½ ounces halved button or cremini mushrooms
⅔ cup crème fraîche or sour cream
1 tablespoon creamed horseradish
2 tablespoons snipped fresh chives

1 Mash and season the potatoes. Whisk in the egg yolks, butter, flour, and milk to give a soft mash.

2 Whisk the egg whites in a clean bowl until stiff peaks form, then fold into the potatoes.

3 Heat a little oil in a large skillet and add large spoonfuls of the batter. Cook for 2 minutes on each side until browned, crisp, and slightly souffléd. Keep warm until ready to serve.

4 Heat the 2 tablespoons of oil in a large skillet. Add the mushrooms and cook over high heat until browned and softened. Add the crème fraîche or sour cream and the creamed horseradish. Stir in the chives, season to taste and serve with the potato pancakes.

Spinach Roulade

Serves 4

6 ounces fresh spinach leaves

$\frac{1}{3}$ stick (3 tablespoons) butter, plus extra for greasing

3 tablespoons all-purpose flour, plus extra for dusting

$1\frac{2}{3}$ cups milk

3 eggs, separated

Salt and freshly ground black pepper

$\frac{1}{4}$ teaspoon freshly grated nutmeg

$\frac{1}{4}$ cup freshly grated Parmesan cheese

6 ounces garlic-and-herb cream cheese

$\frac{1}{3}$ cup ricotta cheese

2 tablespoons sour cream

2 tablespoons snipped fresh chives

1 Preheat the oven to 400°F. Wash the spinach and cook in a covered saucepan for 2–3 minutes until just wilted. Cool slightly, squeeze out all the moisture and finely chop. Grease and line a 9 x 13-inch jelly roll pan with parchment paper. Grease the paper and dust lightly with flour.

2 Melt the butter in a saucepan and stir in the flour. Cook for 1 minute, then remove from the heat. Gradually whisk in the milk, then return to the heat, and continue whisking gently until the mixture boils and thickens. Boil for 1 minute, then remove from the heat once more.

3 Whisk in the egg yolks one at a time until the mixture is smooth. Beat in the spinach, salt, pepper, and nutmeg.

4 Whisk the egg whites in a clean bowl until stiff peaks form and fold into the mixture. Pour the mixture into the pan and spread out evenly. Bake for about 12–14 minutes, or until lightly set.

5 Sprinkle the Parmesan cheese over a sheet of parchment paper and turn the roulade out onto it. Remove the lining paper and let cool slightly. Beat the garlic-and-herb cheese, ricotta, sour cream, and chives together. Spread the mixture over the roulade, then use the paper to roll it up from one long side. Cut into slices before serving.

Menu

Spinach Roulade

~

Carrots with Maple Syrup (p.182)

~

Spiced Grilled Sweet Potatoes (p.170)

Butternut Squash
with Goat Cheese

Serves 2

1 butternut squash, about 2 pounds in
  weight, halved and seeded
Extra virgin olive oil
Salt and freshly ground black pepper
2 scallions, finely chopped
2 tablespoons chopped fresh parsley
4 ounces round mild goat cheese,
  sliced horizontally in half
Green salad, to serve

Menu

Butternut Squash
with Goat Cheese
~
Berry Frozen Treats
(p.214)

1 Preheat the oven to 400°F. Cut two pieces of foil, each large enough to enclose half of the butternut squash. Place the squash halves on the pieces of foil and brush their cut tops generously with olive oil. Sprinkle with salt and pepper, then wrap the foil tightly around the squash to enclose the halves completely. Place on a baking sheet or in an ovenproof dish and bake for 1 hour, or until the squash is completely tender.

2 Remove the squash from the oven and increase the temperature to 425°F. Open the foil and fold it back neatly around the outside of the squash halves. Divide the scallions and parsley between the hollows in the squash halves, and place a slice of goat cheese on top of each.

3 Bake the squash for a further 5-7 minutes, or until the cheese melts and is beginning to brown slightly around the edge. Serve at once with a green salad.

SALADS & SIDE DISHES

- Roasted Corn Salsa
- Tomato Salsa
- Warm Cheese & Smoked Chipotle with Tortilla Chips
- Old-fashioned English Chips
- Luxury Mashed Potatoes
- Duchesse Potatoes
- Patatas Bravas
- Leek & Potato Gratin
- Spiced Grilled Sweet Potatoes
- Latkes
- New England Potato Salad
- Succotash
- Grilled Corn-on-the Cob with Flavored Butter
- Sweet Potato Casserole with Marshmallow Topping
- Braised Fennel

- Braised Sugar Snaps with Lettuce
- Stir-fried Greens with Shiitake Mushrooms
- Fava Beans with Prosciutto
- Potato & Beet Mash
- Carrots with Maple Syrup
- Brussel Sprouts with Sweet Potatoes
- Hot Vegetable Salad
- Spiced Zucchini
- Roasted Vegetables with Pine Nuts & Parmesan
- Cauliflower & Leek Patties
- Maple-baked Acorn Squash
- Mexican Pot Beans
- Classic Coleslaw
- Spinach & Mushroom Salad with Hot Bacon Dressing
- Caesar Salad

- Chickpea & Tomato Salad
- Waldorf Salad
- Chef's Salad
- Panzanella
- Roasted Tomato & Goat Cheese Salad
- Green Bean & Mozzarella Salad
- Stir-fried Brown Rice & Vegetables
- Texas Pilaf
- Broccoli Pilaf
- Coconut Rice
- Egg-fried Rice
- Emmental & Roasted Corn Spoon Bread
- Zucchini Bread
- Old-fashioned Cornbread
- Bacon & Caramelized Onion Rolls

CHAPTER FIVE

SALADS & SIDE DISHES

Roasted Corn Salsa

Serves 4

3 ears corn-on-the cob, husked
1¼ pounds tomatoes, skinned, seeded
    and diced
1 fresh red chile, seeded and finely
    chopped
1 fresh green chile, seeded and
    finely chopped
3 tablespoons olive oil
1 tablespoon chopped fresh parsley
Salt and freshly ground black pepper

1 Preheat a broiler or stovetop grill pan. Put the corn cobs under the broiler or on the grill pan and cook for about 10 minutes, turning them frequently.

2 Let cool, then with a sharp serrated knife remove the kernels. Put the kernels in a bowl. Add the tomatoes, chiles, oil, and parsley and season well with salt and pepper. Mix together and serve.

Tomato Salsa

Serves 4–6

8 plum tomatoes, skinned and chopped
2 tablespoons tomato paste
2 fresh green chiles, such as jalapeño
    or serrano, seeded and chopped
4 scallions, chopped
4 cloves garlic, finely chopped
2 tablespoons chopped fresh cilantro
Grated zest and juice of 1 lime
Salt and freshly ground black pepper
2 teaspoons sugar
¼ cup extra virgin olive oil

1 Mix the tomatoes and tomato paste in a bowl until thoroughly combined. Stir in the chiles, onions, garlic, cilantro, lime zest and juice, sugar, and plenty of salt and pepper. Stir until the sugar and salt have dissolved, then stir in the olive oil.

2 Cover the salsa with plastic wrap or transfer to a plastic storage container and marinate in the refrigerator for at least 4 hours before serving. If possible, make it a day in advance and chill overnight. This is best served lightly chilled.

Warm Cheese & Chipotle
Dip with Tortilla Chips

Serves 4

Vegetable oil, for deep-frying
4 soft flour tortillas, cut into triangles

For the dip
1 tablespoon butter
5 scallions, finely chopped
1 dried chipotle (smoked) chile,
  soaked in hot water for 20 minutes
1¼ cups heavy cream
2½ cups grated cheddar cheese

1 Heat the oil in a large deep saucepan to 375°F and cook the tortillas for 2–3 minutes. Drain on paper towels.

2 Melt the butter in another saucepan. Add the scallion and cook for 5 minutes.

3 Drain the chipotle chile and finely chop. Stir the chile into the onions, then add the cream and cheese. Cook over a low heat until the cheese has melted. Serve warm with the tortilla chips to dip.

Tip
A tortilla is a round, flat unleavened pancake often called 'bread of Mexico'. Cut into triangles, tortillas serve as spoons for dipping.

Old-fashioned

English Chips

Serves 4

6 medium-sized russet potatoes, peeled
Vegetable oil, for deep frying

For the mayonnaise
1 whole egg
2 egg yolks
2 teaspoons English mustard powder
1 tablespoon white wine vinegar
1¼ cups light olive oil or peanut oil
1 tablespoon fresh lemon juice
   (optional)

Tip
To deep-fat fry safely, you should only fill the pan one-third full. Never fry wet potatoes and never leave the pan unattended.

1 Peel the potatoes with a small knife or a vegetable peeler, then using a large chef's knife, cut off the rounded edges to make the potatoes into even rectangles. Cut each potato rectangle into ½inch wide strips, then again lengthwise into chips. Fill a bowl with cold water and drop in the chips as they are made. This removes the starch. Set aside while the oil heats up.

2 Heat the vegetable oil for deep-frying in a deep fat fryer or large saucepan to 325°F. Drain the potatoes well and pat dry on paper towels. Deep-fry in batches for 6–8 minutes, or until soft and pale, transferring to a plate lined with paper towels.

3 Increase the temperature of the oil to 375°F. Re-fry the chips, in batches, for 3–4 minutes until crisp and golden. Drain on paper towels and keep warm.

4 For the mayonnaise, put the egg and egg yolks in a food processor with the mustard and vinegar and process for a few seconds. With the motor running, slowly pour in the olive oil. If it is very thick, blend in the lemon juice. Serve with the chips.

Luxury Mashed Potatoes

Serves 4–6

2¼ pounds potatoes, peeled and halved
Salt and freshly ground white pepper
1¼ cups single cream
⅓ stick (3 tablespoons) butter

1 Put the potatoes in a saucepan and pour in just enough cold water to cover them. Add a little salt, bring to a boil and reduce the heat. Cover the pan and simmer for 15 minutes. Drain well.

2 Return the potatoes to the pan and pour in the cream. Replace the pan on the heat and stir well. Bring to a boil, then simmer for 5 minutes, stirring frequently, until the potatoes are breaking up. Add the butter and plenty of white pepper, then mash until smooth. Remove from the heat, taste for seasoning and serve at once.

Duchesse Potatoes

Serves 4

2¾ pounds russet potatoes, peeled
Salt
½ stick (4 tablespoons) butter, plus
    extra for brushing
½ cup milk
2 egg yolks

1 Halve the potatoes and cook them in a large saucepan of cold salted water. Bring to a boil and cook until tender, then drain well and mash. Heat the butter and milk in another saucepan and pour the mixture over the potatoes. Beat for a couple of minutes with a hand-held electric mixer. Let cool, then mix in the egg yolks.

2 Preheat the oven to 400°F. Spoon the mashed potatoes into a piping bag fitted with a star tip nozzle and pipe out 18 rosettes on a baking sheet. Melt the remaining butter, brush each rosette, then cook in the oven for 20 minutes.

Patatas Bravas

Serves 4

5 potatoes, peeled and cut into
   1-inch cubes
Salt
6 tablespoons olive oil
1 red onion, chopped
3 cloves garlic, chopped
1 tablespoon paprika
Pinch or more of dried red pepper
   flakes
14-ounce can chopped tomatoes
1 tablespoon chopped fresh oregano

1 Parboil the potatoes in a saucepan of boiling salted water for 5 minutes, then drain well.

2 Heat 4 tablespoons of the oil in a large skillet. Add the potatoes and fry slowly for 15 minutes over medium heat. Transfer the potatoes to an ovenproof serving dish and keep warm in a moderate oven.

3 Heat the remaining 2 tablespoons oil in the skillet. Add the onion and garlic and cook for 10 minutes until golden. Add the paprika and pepper flakes and cook for a further 2 minutes. Drain most of the excess juice from the tomatoes, then add them to the fried onion mixture. Cook for 5 minutes, then stir in the oregano. Pour the tomato sauce over the potatoes and serve.

Leek & Potato Gratin

Serves 4

4 large potatoes, thinly sliced
2 teaspoons fennel seeds
3 tablespoons extra virgin olive oil
2 leeks, thinly sliced
3 cloves garlic, chopped
Salt and freshly ground black pepper
6 tomatoes, skinned and thinly sliced
2 tablespoons chopped fresh parsley
2 tablespoons freshly grated Parmesan
   cheese
2 tablespoons plain dry white
   bread crumbs
8 ounces mozzarella cheese, chopped

1 Preheat the oven to 350°F. Put the potatoes in a large saucepan and cover with boiling water. Boil for 2 minutes and drain.

2 Rinse and dry the pan, then place the fennel seeds in it. Roast over a gentle heat until they are aromatic, then add the olive oil, leeks, and garlic with plenty of salt and pepper. Stir the mixture well and cook over medium heat for about 10 minutes, or until the leeks are softened.

3 Put a layer of the boiled potatoes in a deep ovenproof dish. Top with a little of the leek mixture, a layer of tomatoes, and a sprinkling of parsley. Continue layering the potatoes with the leeks and tomatoes until all are used, ending with a layer of potatoes. Cover and cook in the oven for 45 minutes.

4 Mix the Parmesan with the bread crumbs and mozzarella cheese. Sprinkle this evenly over the top of the vegetables and return the dish to the oven, uncovered, for a further 30 minutes, or until the topping is crisp and golden. Let stand to cool slightly for 5 minutes before serving.

Spiced Grilled
Sweet Potatoes

Serves 4

4 medium-size sweet potatoes
2 tablespoons olive oil
1 teaspoon crushed chiles
½ teaspoon ground cinnamon
2 cloves garlic, crushed
Salt and freshly ground black pepper

Tip

Their delicious sweetness makes these potatoes wonderfully versatile, not only in soups and casseroles, but also in sweet dishes, breads, and in puddings.

1 Preheat the gas grill to medium direct heat.

2 Cut the sweet potatoes, without peeling them, lengthwise into 8 wedges each. Put the remaining ingredients into a large bowl and mix together. Season to taste with salt and pepper. Add the potato wedges and mix gently until coated in the spices and oil.

3 Grill the sweet potato wedges, cut-side down over direct heat for 8–10 minutes, turning once, until tender and golden. Watch the potatoes carefully—sweet potatoes can burn very easily because of their high sugar content. Serve immediately.

Latkes

Makes about 24

1½ pounds potatoes, peeled and
  coarsely grated
1 egg, beaten
Salt and freshly ground black pepper
3 tablespoons all-purpose flour
Sunflower oil, for frying
Sour cream or apple sauce, to serve

1 Put the potatoes in a sieve and rinse under cold running water, then squeeze the moisture out of them. Transfer to a bowl, and add the egg with plenty of salt and pepper. Stir in the flour.

2 Heat a little oil in a skillet. Stir the potato mixture, then put a spoonful in the pan, and quickly spread the grated potatoes into an evenly thick round. Repeat with more mixture, adding as many latkes as will comfortably fit in the pan with a little space in between.

3 Cook over medium heat until the latkes are crisp and golden underneath. Turn and cook the other side until crisp and golden. Use a spatula to remove the latkes from the pan, and drain individually on paper towels. Keep the latkes hot until all the remaining mixture is cooked. Serve with sour cream or apple sauce.

New England

Potato Salad

Serves 4

1½ pounds waxy new potatoes, halved
  if large
Salt and freshly ground black pepper
3 ribs celery, finely diced
2 scallions, finely sliced
1 red bell pepper, seeded and finely
  diced
½ cup mayonnaise
⅔ cup sour cream
2 tablespoons chopped fresh parsley

1 Cook the potatoes in a large saucepan of boiling salted water for 15–20 minutes until just soft. Drain well and cut into small pieces. Put in a large bowl with the celery, scallions, and pepper.

2 Mix the mayonnaise with the sour cream and season with salt and pepper, then spoon the mixture over the potato salad. Mix well until all the ingredients are thoroughly coated and lightly stir in the parsley. Chill until ready to serve.

Succotash

Serves 6–8

1 cup dried butter beans, soaked
    overnight in cold water
$\frac{1}{4}$ stick (2 tablespoons) butter
4 thick bacon slices, chopped
1 large onion, halved and thinly sliced
1 green bell pepper, seeded and
    chopped
3 cups sweetcorn kernels (fresh or
    frozen)
$\frac{1}{2}$ cup chicken or vegetable broth
Salt and freshly ground black pepper
$\frac{1}{4}$ cup light cream
2 tablespoons chopped fresh cilantro

Tip
Butter beans are sweet
with a soft, floury texture
when cooked. They are very
good added to mixed bean
salads and rich, meaty
stews.

1 Drain the beans and put them in a large saucepan. Add plenty of water and bring to a boil, then boil for 10 minutes. Reduce the heat, cover the pan and simmer the beans for 40 minutes, or until they are tender. Drain in a colander.

2 Add the butter and bacon to the pan and cook until the bacon has just changed color. Stir in the onion and pepper and cook for 10 minutes, or until the onion is softened, but not browned. Stir frequently during cooking.

3 Add the corn and the broth, then bring to a boil and reduce the heat. Cover the pan and simmer the corn for 3 minutes. Add the drained beans but do not mix them in. Cover the pan and simmer for a further 5 minutes, or until the corn becomes tender.

4 Add salt and pepper to taste and mix the corn and beans. Stir in the cream and heat for a few seconds without boiling, then add the cilantro and mix lightly. Serve at once.

Grilled Corn-on-the-Cob

with Flavored Butter

Serves 4

1 stick (8 tablespoons) unsalted butter, softened

1 hot green chile, seeded and finely chopped

$1/2$ teaspoon ground cumin

1 teaspoon ground coriander

2 tablespoons chopped fresh cilantro, plus cilantro leaves to garnish

Salt and freshly ground black pepper

8 ears fresh corns, husks intact

Tip

If you cannot find husked corn, wrap the corn in foil after spreading with butter.

1 Preheat the gas grill to medium direct heat.

2 Put the butter into a medium bowl and beat with a fork or wooden spoon until smooth. Add the chile, cumin, coriander, chopped cilantro, and salt and pepper. Mix together thoroughly. Set aside.

3 Carefully peel back the corn husks, without removing them. Pull off the silk threads, removing as much as possible. Spread each cob with about 2 tablespoons of the butter mixture, then carefully fold the husk back up over each cob. Tie securely with string at the top.

4 Grill the corn over direct medium heat for 8-10 minutes, turning occasionally, until the corn is lightly and evenly browned.

5 Peel off the husks, garnish with cilantro leaves and serve at once.

Sweet Potato Casserole

with Marshmallow Topping

Serves 6

8 medium sweet potatoes
¼ cup dark brown sugar
¼ stick (2 tablespoons) butter
Freshly grated nutmeg, to taste
¾ teaspoon ground cinnamon
¾ teaspoon ground allspice
Freshly squeezed juice of ½ orange
Salt and freshly ground black pepper
Marshmallows, for topping

1 Peel the sweet potatoes and put them in a large saucepan or casserole. Cover with cold water and bring to a boil over a high heat. Reduce the heat to medium and simmer for about 30 minutes, or until the potatoes are tender. Drain and transfer to a large bowl.

2 Meanwhile, preheat the oven to 375°F. Using a potato masher, mash the potatoes until smooth. Alternatively, put the potatoes through a potato ricer or food mill, or beat with a hand-held electric mixer. Add the sugar, butter, nutmeg to taste, cinnamon, allspice, orange juice, and salt and pepper, and beat until smooth and well blended.

3 Spoon the mixture into a 3-quart baking dish and arrange the marshmallows in rows across the surface, pressing them gently into the potato mixture. Bake for 10–15 minutes, or until the potatoes are bubbling and the marshmallows are golden and soft.

Braised Fennel

Serves 4

¼ stick (2 tablespoons) butter
1 small onion, finely chopped
1 small carrot, finely chopped
Salt and freshly ground black pepper
4 bulbs fennel, halved lengthwise
2 cups medium dry white wine

1 Preheat the oven to 400°F. Melt the butter in a casserole. Add the onion and carrot, season with salt and pepper and cook, stirring, for 5 minutes.

2 Add the fennel to the casserole, flat-side down and cook for 2 minutes, then pour in the wine. Heat until simmering, basting the fennel with the wine. Cover and transfer to the oven. Cook about 40 minutes, turning the fennel after 30 minutes, until the bulbs are completely tender. Taste and adjust the seasoning before serving.

Tip
Fennel has a pronounced aniseed flavor—grill meat or fish on top of the leaves so that the fragrance is absorbed as the meat cooks.

Braised Sugar Snaps
with Lettuce

Serves 4

¼ stick (2 tablespoons) butter
1 small onion, finely chopped
2 tablespoons chopped fresh tarragon
1 pound sugar snap peas
Salt and freshly ground black pepper
½ cup medium-dry white wine
1 small Little Gem lettuce heart, finely shredded
1 spring onion, finely chopped
4 large fresh basil sprigs

1 Melt the butter in a large saucepan. Add the onion, stir well and cover the pan. Cook gently for 5 minutes, then stir in the tarragon and sugar snap peas. Add salt and pepper to taste, and stir in the wine. Heat until just simmering, then cover the pan and cook gently for 5 minutes.

2 Stir in the shredded lettuce, cover the pan again and simmer for a further 3 minutes, or until the lettuce has just wilted and the peas are tender, but still crisp.

3 Taste the sugar snap peas and add more seasoning if necessary, then stir in the spring onion. Use scissors to shred the basil sprigs into the pan, cutting them finely and including the soft stalks with the leaves. Immediately remove from the heat and serve at once, stirring well so that the basil is thoroughly blended into the vegetables as they are served.

Stir-fried Greens
with Shiitake Mushrooms

Serves 4–6

1 tablespoon vegetable oil

3 scallions, sliced

1-inch piece fresh ginger, peeled and
   finely chopped

3 cloves garlic, crushed

12 shiitake mushrooms, sliced

¼ cup light soy sauce

1 tablespoon honey or sugar

1 teaspoon toasted sesame oil

3 tablespoons rice wine or sherry

2 pounds fresh mixed greens (such as
   spinach, mustard greens, collard
   greens, bok choy or Swiss chard),
   stems discarded

1 teaspoon toasted sesame seeds, to
   garnish

1 Heat the oil in a wok or large skillet. Add half the scallions, the ginger, and garlic and stir-fry for 1 minute. Add the mushrooms and stir-fry for 2 minutes. Add the soy sauce, honey or sugar, sesame oil, and rice wine or sherry, and bring to a boil. Cook for 1 minute.

2 Add the mixed greens and stir-fry for about 30 seconds until they become slightly wilted. Using a slotted spoon, remove the vegetables from the wok and transfer to a serving dish.

3 Pour any sauce left in the wok or pan over the vegetables. Sprinkle with the remaining scallions and the sesame seeds and serve.

Fava Beans
with Prosciutto

Serves 4

4 fresh savory or thyme sprigs

Salt and freshly ground black pepper

3 pounds young fava beans, shelled
(they yield just over 1 pound beans)

1 tablespoon extra virgin olive oil

4 ounces prosciutto, cut into fine strips

2 tablespoons mild onion

2 tablespoons chopped fresh savory or
thyme leaves

Lemon wedges, to serve (optional)

Tip
Savory and fava beans go well together—they are often grown next to each other as the herb helps to keep away blackflies.

1 Place the savory or thyme sprigs in a saucepan of salted water and bring to a boil. Add the fava beans. Bring back to a boil and cook for about 5 minutes, or until the beans are tender.

2 Meanwhile, heat the olive oil in a nonstick skillet. Sprinkle the strips of prosciutto evenly over the pan and cook for about 2 minutes, until the prosciutto is crisp. Transfer the prosciutto and its cooking oil to a large serving bowl. Add the onion and savory or thyme leaves.

3 Drain the beans, discard the herb sprigs, then add them to the prosciutto. Mix well, then add a little salt, if necessary, and plenty of freshly ground black pepper. Toss well and serve at once.

4 Offer lemon wedges with the beans if they are served as the main dish for a light meal or first course, so that the juice can be added to taste.

Potato & Beet Mash

Serves 4–6

2¼ pounds potatoes, peeled and cut
   into chunks
Salt and freshly ground black pepper
Butter, to taste
¼ cup plain yogurt
1 pound cooked beets, coarsely grated
1 small onion, very finely chopped

1 Cook the potatoes in a large saucepan of boiling salted water for about 10 minutes, or until tender. Drain well, then return to the pan.

2 Add butter to taste and the yogurt, then mash until smooth. Beat in the grated beet and chopped onion, then return the pan to the heat and stir for 2–3 minutes until thoroughly reheated. Add salt and pepper to taste and serve at once.

Carrots

with Maple Syrup

Serves 4

¼ stick (2 tablespoons) butter
About ½ cup water
8 carrots, cut into even-sized pieces,
   about 2 inches long
2 tablespoons pure maple syrup
Small bunch of fresh parsley, finely
   chopped

1 Melt the butter in a large saucepan and pour in the water. You need roughly ½ inch in the bottom of the pan. Add the carrots and stir well to coat them in liquid. Cover and simmer for 12–15 minutes.

2 Remove the lid, increase the heat and bubble to reduce the liquid to about 2 tablespoons. Add the maple syrup, stir and bubble for 1 minute. Stir in the chopped parsley and serve immediately.

Brussel Sprouts
with Sweet Potatoes

Serves 4

1 pound sweet potatoes, peeled
$3/_4$ pound small Brussels sprouts
Salt and freshly ground black pepper
2 tablespoons extra virgin olive oil
Pinch of ground cloves
Good pinch of ground mace
$1/_2$ teaspoon dried oregano or
   marjoram
1 teaspoon sugar
Grated zest and juice of 1 large orange

1 Cut the sweet potato into chunks about the same size as the Brussels sprouts. Add the sweet potatoes to a large saucepan of boiling salted water and bring back just to boiling point. Cook for 2 minutes.

2 Add the Brussels sprouts to the pan and bring back to a boil. Reduce the heat, if necessary, so that the water does not boil too fiercely and break up the sweet potato, then cook for 5 minutes until the sweet potato and sprouts are tender, but not too soft. Drain in a colander.

3 Return the pan to the heat and add the olive oil, herbs and spices, sugar, and orange zest and juice. Whisk over a high heat until the mixture boils. Boil hard, still whisking, for about 30 seconds. Add salt and pepper to taste.

4 Remove the pan from the heat and return the vegetables to it. Carefully turn them in the orange mixture to coat them evenly, taking care not to break up the delicate pieces of sweet potato and the sprouts. Serve immediately.

Hot Vegetable Salad

Serves 4

28 small new potatoes, scrubbed
Salt and freshly ground black pepper
16 baby carrots, scrubbed
1 cup fresh or frozen peas
Handful of fresh parsley sprigs
Handful of fresh mint sprigs
Handful of fresh dill sprigs
1 teaspoon sugar
1 tablespoon whole-grain mustard
2 tablespoons balsamic vinegar
5 tablespoons extra virgin olive oil
8 scallions, chopped
1–2 romaine lettuce hearts, shredded

1 Put the potatoes in a large saucepan and pour in boiling water to cover. Add a little salt, then bring to a boil. Reduce the heat, cover and simmer for 10 minutes. Add the carrots and peas and bring back to a boil, then reduce the heat again. Cover and keep the vegetables just boiling for a further 5 minutes until the potatoes and vegetables are cooked.

2 Meanwhile, place the parsley, mint, dill, and sugar in a food processor and process until finely chopped. Add the mustard, vinegar, salt and pepper, then process again until well mixed. Pour in the olive oil and process for a few seconds. Turn into a bowl and stir in the scallions.

3 Drain the vegetables and add them to the dressing, then toss well to coat them evenly. Arrange the lettuce in a large shallow dish and pile in the vegetable salad. Serve at once.

Spiced Zucchini

Serves 4

¼ stick (2 tablespoons) butter
1 onion, finely chopped
8 green cardamom pods
2 teaspoons cumin seeds
1 bay leaf
1½ pounds zucchini, peeled, halved,
   and seeded, cut into 1-inch chunks
Salt and freshly ground black pepper
1 cup coconut milk
½ cup Greek yogurt or crème fraîche
2 scallions, finely chopped
2 tablespoons chopped fresh cilantro

1 Melt the butter in a saucepan. Add the onion. Add the cardamom, making a slit in each pod and crushing it slightly as you add it to the pan. Stir in the cumin seeds and bay leaf, then cover the pan, and cook gently for 15 minutes.

2 Stir in the zucchini with salt and pepper to taste. Continue stirring until the zucchini are thoroughly combined with the onion and spices. Then pour in the coconut milk and heat until simmering. Simmer, uncovered, for 15 minutes, or until the zucchini are tender. Stir the zucchini frequently so that the pieces cook evenly.

3 Stir in the yogurt or crème fraîche and immediately remove the pan from the heat. Add more seasoning, if necessary. Remove the bay leaf and serve immediately, sprinkled with the scallions and fresh cilantro.

Roasted Vegetables
with Pine Nuts & Parmesan

Serves 4

¼ cup olive oil
8 small new potatoes, halved or
   quartered lengthwise, if large
4 small parsnips, halved or quartered
   lengthwise, if large
Salt and freshly ground black pepper
6 baby leeks, trimmed
4 asparagus spears, trimmed
½ cup freshly grated Parmesan cheese
2 tablespoons pine nuts, toasted
2 tablespoons fresh white bread
   crumbs

1 Preheat the oven to 400°F. Pour the oil into a roasting pan, add the potatoes and parsnips and toss well to coat in the oil. Season with salt and pepper and roast in the oven for 30 minutes.

2 Add the leeks and asparagus to the roasting pan. Toss all the vegetables together, return to the oven and roast for a further 25 minutes.

3 Mix together the Parmesan cheese, pine nuts, and bread crumbs.

4 Sprinkle the mixture over the roasted vegetables and cook for a further 5 minutes until crispy and golden.

Cauliflower & Leek

Patties

Makes 8 patties

2 tablespoons olive oil
2 leeks, finely chopped
1 clove garlic, crushed
1 teaspoon dried marjoram
3/4 pound cauliflower (including the stalk and any little green leaves), finely chopped
Salt and freshly ground black pepper
1 cup fresh white bread crumbs
2 tablespoons chopped fresh parsley
4 scallions, chopped
3/4 cup grated cheddar cheese

1 Heat the oil in a saucepan. Add the leeks, garlic, and marjoram. Stir for 5 minutes, or until the leeks are softened slightly, then add the cauliflower and stir well. Cover and cook for 5 minutes. Stir in the seasoning, then cook, uncovered, for a further 5 minutes, stirring occasionally. Turn the vegetables into a bowl and let cool.

2 Mix in the bread crumbs, parsley, scallions, and cheese. Taste for seasoning and add more salt and pepper, if required. Cover a baking sheet with plastic wrap, shape the mixture into 8 round patties and place them on the baking sheet as they are ready. Cover loosely with plastic wrap and chill for 1 hour.

3 Preheat the broiler. Place the patties on a flameproof dish, or line the broiler pan with foil and brush it lightly with oil, then place the patties on it. Brush the patties with a little oil and broil for 3-4 minutes, or until golden brown on top. Turn the patties, brush with oil and cook until golden for 3-4 minutes on the second side. Serve at once.

Maple-baked Acorn Squash

Serves 4

2 medium acorn squash

¼ stick (2 tablespoons) butter

¼ cup pure maple syrup

¼ teaspoon salt

¼ teaspoon ground cinnamon

⅛ teaspoon ground allspice

¼ cup chopped pecans or walnuts (optional)

Tip

Acorn squash can make a delicious and easy-to-make holiday treat—simply stuff them with prepared mincemeat.

1 Preheat the oven to 350°F. Cut each squash in half lengthwise, then scoop out their seeds and fibers. Use a sharp knife to slice off a small piece of each base. Arrange the squash halves, cut-side down, in an ovenproof dish and cover with foil. Bake for about 30 minutes, or until the squash begins to soften.

2 Turn the squash cut-side up and divide the butter, maple syrup, salt and spices equally among them. Sprinkle each one with nuts, if using. Bake, uncovered, for about 20 minutes, or until the squash are tender.

Mexican Pot Beans

Serves 4–6

1 pound dried pinto beans
1 onion, finely chopped
2½ ounces smoked bacon, chopped
2 dried red chiles, roughly chopped
2 cloves garlic, roughly chopped
1 bay leaf, crumbled
1 tablespoon salt
Freshly ground black pepper, to taste

1 Put the pinto beans into a large bowl and pick them over, removing any little stones or beans that are shrivelled or discolored. Cover the beans with at least twice their volume of cold water and let soak overnight.

2 Next day, drain the beans and put into a large saucepan (one that is tall and deep is best as it will reduce evaporation of water). Add the onion, bacon, chiles, garlic, and bay leaf and cover with water by about 3-4 inches (about 3-4 quarts).

3 Bring slowly to a boil, skimming off any residue that rises to the surface. When boiling, reduce the heat, cover and simmer very gently for 2 hours.

4 Add the salt and continue to cook the beans, uncovered, for another 1 hour, or until they are very tender and the liquid is very thick. Taste for seasoning and add more salt, if necessary, and black pepper. Serve immediately or cool and refrigerate for up to 3 days.

Classic Coleslaw

Serves 4

²/₃ cup mayonnaise

²/₃ cup plain yogurt or crème fraîche

1 teaspoon Dijon mustard

Salt and freshly ground black pepper

3 tablespoons chopped fresh parsley

3 tablespoons raisins

¹/₂ pound green cabbage, finely
  shredded

1 large carrot, coarsely grated

¹/₂ small onion, finely chopped

1 First make the mayonnaise dressing in a large bowl, big enough to mix the salad. Mix the mayonnaise with the yogurt or crème fraîche. Add the mustard, plenty of salt and pepper, and the parsley. Stir well so that all the flavors are fully blended.

2 Add the raisins to the dressing and mix well. Then add the cabbage, carrot, and onion. Mix the ingredients thoroughly until they are combined and coated with dressing. Taste and add salt and pepper as necessary.

3 Cover the coleslaw and chill for at least 1 hour, then remove from the refrigerator for 15-20 minutes before serving. The salad tastes best when made and chilled a day in advance—the flavors mingle and mellow, and the raisins plump up and impart a gentle sweetness to the salad.

Spinach & Mushroom
Salad with Hot Bacon Dressing

Serves 4

1 pound baby spinach leaves, washed
and dried

4 ounces white mushrooms, thinly
sliced

1 tablespoon vegetable oil or bacon fat

4 slices bacon, cut into thin shreds

4 scallions, thinly sliced,
or 2 tablespoons snipped chives

1 clove garlic, crushed

½ cup cider vinegar or wine vinegar

½ teaspoon salt

½ teaspoon dry mustard powder

Freshly ground black pepper, to taste

1 Toss the spinach leaves and sliced mushrooms in a large, heatproof salad bowl. Heat the oil or bacon fat in a heavy-based frying-pan over medium heat. Add the bacon and cook until crisp and brown, stirring frequently. Drain on paper towels.

2 Add the scallions and garlic to the pan and cook over a low heat until softened, stirring frequently. Stir in the vinegar, salt and dry mustard, and season with black pepper. Bring to a boil, and carefully pour over the leaves. Sprinkle the bacon on top and toss lightly to mix. Serve immediately.

Caesar Salad

Serves 6

1 egg, at room temperature
4–7 tablespoons olive oil
1 tablespoon butter
1 clove garlic, crushed
3–4 ounces French bread, cut into
   small cubes
2 tablespoons lemon juice
Freshly ground black pepper, to taste
1 large or 2 small heads romaine
   lettuce, torn into bite-sized pieces
3/4 cup freshly grated Parmesan cheese,
   plus long curls or shreds to garnish
3 anchovy fillets, cut up (optional)

1 To coddle the egg, bring a small saucepan of water to a boil over a high heat. Carefully slide the whole egg into the water and remove the pan from the heat. Cover and let stand for 1 minute.

2 Heat 1–2 tablespoons oil and the butter in a medium skillet over a medium-high heat. Add the garlic and bread cubes and cook for 2–3 minutes, tossing and stirring, until the bread is golden on all sides. Remove from the heat and set the croûtons aside.

3 Put the lemon juice in a large salad bowl and add 3–5 tablespoons oil. Crack the egg into the bowl and whisk it into the lemon juice and oil until blended and creamy. Season with pepper, then add the lettuce and grated Parmesan and toss to coat. Add the anchovies, if using. Sprinkle over the croûtons. Garnish with Parmesan curls or shreds and serve.

Chickpea & Tomato
Salad

Serves 3–4

1 clove garlic, crushed
Juice of 1 lemon
1 tablespoon tahini
3 tablespoons extra virgin olive oil
2 tablespoons chopped fresh mint
2 tablespoons chopped fresh cilantro
1 tablespoon chopped fresh parsley
12 cherry tomatoes, halved
1 small red onion, finely chopped
14-ounce can chickpeas, rinsed
Salt and freshly ground black pepper

1 Whisk the garlic, lemon juice, tahini, olive oil, and chopped herbs together in a medium bowl.

2 Stir in the tomatoes, onion and chickpeas, and season to taste with salt and pepper.

Tip
Chickpeas have a rich, nutty flavor and are ideal in casseroles, soups and stews, as well as providing body for salads.

Waldorf Salad

Serves 4

4 ribs celery, thinly sliced

2 large red apples, quartered, cored, and diced

1 cup walnuts, chopped

³/₄ cup chopped soft dates or figs (optional)

About 1 cup mayonnaise

Lettuce leaves

Walnut halves or apple slices, to garnish

1 Combine the celery, apples, and walnuts in a bowl, and the dates or figs, if using. Gradually stir in enough mayonnaise to hold all the ingredients together.

2 Arrange the lettuce leaves on a plate and heap the salad on them. Garnish with walnut halves or apple slices.

Chef's Salad

Serves 4

2 heads Boston or butterhead lettuce, trimmed

8 ounces honey-baked ham, cut into strips

8 ounces cooked chicken or turkey breast, cut into strips

8 ounces Emmental or cheddar cheese, cut into strips

8 cherry tomatoes, quartered

4 hard-boiled eggs, quartered

For the dressing

2 tablespoons lemon juice or white wine vinegar

1 tablespoon Dijon mustard

Salt and freshly ground black pepper

1 clove garlic, crushed

1 teaspoon sugar (optional)

$1/4$ cup vegetable oil

2–3 tablespoons extra virgin olive oil

1 To make the dressing, put the lemon juice or white wine vinegar in a small bowl with the mustard, salt and pepper, garlic, and sugar, if using. Stir to blend well. Slowly pour in the vegetable oil in a thin stream, whisking continuously until a smooth, creamy dressing begins to form. Continue whisking while adding the olive oil in the same way until the dressing is thick and smooth. Set aside.

2 Leave any small lettuce leaves whole and tear large leaves into smaller pieces, then divide evenly among 4 individual salad bowls or place on a large shallow platter.

3 Arrange the ham, chicken or turkey, and cheese strips on top of the lettuce, radiating from the middle to resemble wheel spokes and keeping even spaces between each ingredient. Fill the spaces with the tomato and egg quarters. Drizzle the salad dressing over and serve.

Panzanella

Serves 6–8

1 small ciabatta or rustic loaf, about
   6 ounces, cut into cubes
1 cucumber, peeled, seeded and
   coarsely chopped
4 vine-ripened tomatoes, halved and
   cut into chunks
2 tablespoons capers, rinsed

For the dressing
2 cloves garlic
2 tablespoons red wine vinegar
$\frac{1}{2}$ cup olive oil
Salt and freshly ground black pepper
2 hard-boiled eggs, coarsely chopped
8–10 fresh basil leaves

1 Preheat the oven to 400°F. Place the bread cubes on a baking sheet and toast in the oven for 10 minutes. Transfer to a high-sided salad bowl.

2 Add the cucumber and tomatoes to the salad bowl. Sprinkle with the capers.

3 To make the dressing, pound the garlic cloves in a mortar with a pestle. Whisk in the vinegar and oil, and season with salt and pepper. Pour the dressing over the salad.

4 Arrange the hard-boiled eggs on top of the salad with the basil leaves. Let stand for 15 minutes, then stir once before serving—you want the bread to soak up the juices and dressing but not become unappealingly soggy.

Roasted Tomato &

Goat Cheese Salad

Serves 4–6

6 plum tomatoes, halved lengthwise
¼ cup olive oil
1 teaspoon chopped fresh rosemary
2 tablespoons chopped fresh basil,
   plus extra to garnish
1 tablespoon balsamic vinegar
1 shallot, finely chopped
Salt and freshly ground black pepper
3½ ounces fresh goat cheese
Bread, to serve

1 Preheat the broiler to high. Arrange the tomato halves, cut-side up, on a broiler pan or baking sheet. Mix 1 tablespoon of the oil with the rosemary. Brush this mixture over the tomatoes. Transfer to the broiler and cook for 6–8 minutes until the tomatoes are softened and starting to char round the edges. Remove from the heat and transfer the tomatoes to a large serving dish with any juices.

2 Mix the remaining oil with the basil, balsamic vinegar, and shallot. Pour this mixture over the tomatoes and season with some salt and pepper. Cool to room temperature.

3 Divide the tomatoes among 4 or 6 serving plates and top each one with a spoonful of goat cheese, drizzling over some of the dressing. Garnish with some fresh basil leaves and serve with plenty of bread.

Green Bean &

Mozzarella Salad

Serves 4

¾ **pound thin green beans**
¾ **pound fresh mozzarella cheese,**
   thinly sliced

For the dressing
3 tablespoons coriander seeds
Grated zest and juice of 1 large orange
1 tablespoon cider vinegar
½ teaspoon sugar
1 teaspoon whole-grain mustard
1 small clove garlic, chopped
Salt and freshly ground black pepper
5 tablespoons extra virgin olive oil
3 tablespoons chopped fresh parsley

1 To make the dressing, roast the coriander seeds in a small, heavy-based saucepan over a medium heat. Shake the pan frequently until the seeds begin to smell aromatic and darken very slightly. Tip the coriander seeds into a mortar as soon as they are roasted—do not leave them in the pan or they may overcook, becoming dark and bitter. Use a pestle to crush the seeds coarsely.

2 In a bowl large enough to hold the beans, mix the seeds with the orange zest and juice, cider vinegar, sugar, mustard, and garlic. Season with salt and pepper. Whisk until the sugar and salt have dissolved, then whisk in the olive oil to make a slightly thickened dressing. Add the parsley.

3 Cook the green beans in a large saucepan of boiling water for about 3 minutes until crisp but not soft. Drain and immediately add them to the dressing. Turn the beans in the dressing to cool them quickly. Cover and marinate for about 1 hour, if possible, or at least until they are cold.

4 Add the mozzarella to the beans and mix the salad gently, taking care not to break up the cheese. Spoon on to individual plates and serve.

Stir-fried Brown Rice
& Vegetables

Serves 6

2¼ cups short-grain brown rice
4½ cups old water
Pinch of salt
1 cup sesame seeds
Small handful of dried arame seaweed
Sesame oil
2 onions, finely diced
2 teaspoons soy sauce
2 carrots, sliced into matchsticks
¼-inch strips nori seaweed or finely
    chopped fresh parsley, to garnish

1 Wash the rice under cold running water, to allow any debris or chaff to overflow. Combine the rice with the cold water and salt in a heavy-based saucepan. Bring to a rapid boil without the lid, then cover and reduce the heat. Cook for 30–35 minutes until tender.

2 Meanwhile, wash the sesame seeds in a sieve under cold running water, then empty into a heavy-base skillet and cook over a medium heat, stirring, until they turn golden brown and a few of them begin to pop and crackle. Remove and let cool.

3 Soak the arame seaweed in a bowl of water for 5–6 minutes. Remove the arame from the water and squeeze out any excess liquid.

4 Cover the surface of a clean heavy-based skillet with sesame oil and heat. Add the onions with half the soy sauce and sauté until they are translucent. Add the carrots and continue to stir. Add the arame seaweed to the onions and carrots then stir-fry 2 minutes.

5 Slowly add the cooked brown rice to the pan and stir to prevent the mixture from sticking. If you feel the dish needs more liquid, add the water used for soaking the arame. Continue stirring until the rice is hot. Add the remaining soy sauce during the final minute, and mix in the sesame seeds. Garnish with nori seaweed or finely chopped parsley and serve immediately.

Texas Pilaf

Serves 4

1²/₃ cups basmati or Texmati rice
1 tablespoon olive oil
1 onion, finely chopped
1 green chile, seeded and finely
  chopped
1 clove garlic, finely chopped
2 teaspoons cumin seeds
1 large vine-ripened tomato, skinned
  and roughly chopped
2 cups chicken broth
2 tablespoons chopped fresh cilantro
Salt and freshly ground black pepper,
  to taste

1 Put the rice into a large bowl. Pour in plenty of cold water, then swirl the grains gently, let them settle and pour off the cloudy water. Repeat this process several times until the water runs clear. Put the rice into a sieve and let drain while you prepare the remaining ingredients.

2 Heat the oil in a large saucepan or casserole with a tight-fitting lid over medium heat. When hot, add the onion, chile, and garlic. Cook, stirring occasionally, for 5–7 minutes until the onion begins to brown. Add the cumin seeds and stir for a further 30 seconds or so.

3 Add the tomato and cook for another 1 minute until softened. Add the drained rice and stir well to coat in the oil and tomato.

4 Add the broth and bring to a boil. Reduce the heat as low as possible and cover tightly. Simmer over the lowest heat for 15 minutes, then remove from the heat and let stand without lifting the lid for a further 10 minutes.

5 Just before serving, add the cilantro and season to taste with salt and pepper.

Broccoli Pilaf

Serves 4

1 cup basmati rice
16 ounces small broccoli florets
2 tablespoons sunflower oil
2 onions, thinly sliced
2 cloves garlic, crushed
2 ribs celery, thinly sliced
2 tablespoons cumin seeds
8 green cardamom pods
1 bay leaf
1 cinnamon stick
Salt and freshly ground black pepper
1 teaspoon saffron threads
2 tablespoons boiling water

1 Put the basmati rice in a bowl. Pour in plenty of cold water, then swirl the grains gently, let them settle and pour off the cloudy water. Repeat this process several times until the water runs clear. Cover with fresh cold water and set aside to soak for 30 minutes.

2 Cook the broccoli in a large saucepan of boiling water for 2 minutes. Drain the broccoli, reserving the vegetable broth.

3 Heat the oil in a skillet. Add the onions, garlic, celery, cumin seeds, cardamom pods, bay leaf, and cinnamon stick. Stir, then cook 10 minutes stirring occasionally, until the onions have softened and are beginning to brown.

4 Meanwhile, drain the rice and set it aside in the sieve. When the onions are cooked, add the rice to the pan and pour in the reserved broth. Add salt and pepper, then bring to a boil over high heat and stir once. Cover the pan and reduce the heat to the lowest setting. Cook for 10 minutes.

5 While the rice is cooking, pound the saffron threads in a mortar with a pestle and stir in the boiling water. Sprinkle the saffron water over the rice, then add the broccoli, leaving it piled on top of the rice. Quickly re-cover the pan and cook for another 5 minutes. Remove from the heat and let stand, without removing the lid, for 3 minutes. Fluff the rice with a fork and mix in the broccoli. Serve immediately.

Coconut Rice

Serves 4

1³/₄ cups Thai jasmine rice
1²/₃ cups coconut milk
¹/₂ cup water
1 teaspoon salt

1 Put the rice into a large bowl. Pour in plenty of cold water, then swirl the grains gently, let them settle and pour off the cloudy water. Repeat this process several times until the water runs clear. Put the rice into a sieve and leave to drain.

2 Put the rice into a large saucepan with the coconut milk and water. Add the salt and stir well. Cover and bring to a boil. As soon as the liquid comes up to a boil, reduce the heat as low as possible and cook for 10 minutes.

3 Remove from the heat and let stand for a further 10 minutes. Do not lift the lid until the entire 20 minutes have elapsed. Fluff up with a fork before serving.

Egg-fried Rice

Serves 4

1 tablespoon vegetable oil
4 cups cold cooked rice
2 ounces chopped bacon
1 cup thawed frozen peas
8 eggs, beaten
8 tablespoons soy sauce
8 scallions, finely chopped

1 Heat a wok over a high heat until smoking. Add the oil and swirl around the pan. Add the cold cooked rice and stir-fry for 1 minute.

2 Add the bacon and peas. Continue to cook for 5 minutes. Add the eggs and cook for a further 2 minutes. Add the soy sauce and remove from the heat. Stir in the scallions and serve immediately.

Emmental & Roasted
Corn Spoon Bread

Serves 4

2 ears fresh corn-on-the-cob, husked
2 tablespoons vegetable oil
1 cup all-purpose flour
1 cup cornmeal
1 tablespoon baking powder
$^1/_2$ teaspoon baking soda
$^1/_2$ teaspoon salt
2 eggs
1 cup buttermilk
$^1/_2$ stick (4 tablespoons) butter, melted
3 tablespoons grated Emmental cheese

1 Preheat the oven to 400°F. Put the corn cobs in a roasting pan and pour over the oil. Roast in the oven for 30 minutes. Let cool, then slice off the kernels.

2 Mix the flour, cornmeal, baking powder, baking soda, and salt together in a large bowl.

3 Add the eggs and buttermilk and beat well. Stir in the melted butter, Emmental and corn kernels.

4 Preheat the oven to 375°F. Grease and line a 9 x 5 x 3-inch loaf pan and line the bottom with waxed paper. Spoon the mixture into the prepared pan and bake in the oven for 40–45 minutes, or until a skewer inserted into the center comes out clean. Set aside for 10 minutes then turn out on to a wire rack. Serve just warm.

Zucchini Bread

Makes one loaf

3¼ cups all-purpose flour
1 teaspoon salt
2 teaspoons baking powder
2 teaspoons dried thyme
1 zucchini, coarsely grated
  (to yield about 2–2½ cups)
3 eggs
¼ cup extra virgin olive oil
4–6 tablespoons milk

Tip
Zucchini are wonderfully versatile and can be thinly sliced and quickly fried in olive oil. It is also delicious sliced, battered and fried.

1 Preheat the oven to 350°F and grease a 9 x 5-inch loaf pan. Mix the flour, salt, baking powder, and thyme together in a bowl. Make a large well in the middle and add the grated zucchini. Make another well in the middle of the zucchini, but do not mix in.

2 Add the eggs, olive oil, and 4 tablespoons of the milk to the well in the zucchini. Beat the eggs with the wet ingredients and gradually work in the zucchini. Then work in the dry ingredients from the outside of the bowl, adding the remaining 2 tablespoons of milk, if necessary, to make a firm mixture that is also soft enough to drop from the spoon when jerked sharply.

3 Turn the mixture into the loaf pan and press down into the corners. Bake for 45–50 minutes, or until the loaf is well risen and browned on top. Insert a metal skewer into the middle of the bread. If the skewer comes out clean, with no mixture clinging to it, the loaf is cooked. If not, cook for a further 5 minutes and test it again. Turn the loaf out to cool on a wire rack. Serve warm or cool, with butter.

Old-fashioned Cornbread

Serves 6–8

1 stick (8 tablespoons) butter, cut into
cubes
1¼ cups yellow cornmeal
¾ cup all-purpose flour
¼ cup sugar
1 tablespoon baking powder
½ teaspoon salt
1 egg, lightly beaten
1 cup buttermilk
Butter, to serve

1 Preheat the oven to 425°F. Put the butter in a
9–10-inch cast-iron skillet or heavy-based
ovenproof dish and put in the oven for 3–5 minutes
until the butter has melted. Swirl to coat the inside
of the pan.

2 Meanwhile, put the cornmeal, flour, sugar,
baking powder, and salt in a large mixing bowl
and stir to combine. Make a large well in the middle
of the mixture.

3 Set aside 2 tablespoons of the melted butter
in a small bowl to cool slightly and pour the
remainder into the middle of the dry ingredients.
Keep the skillet or dish warm. Using a fork, beat
the egg and buttermilk together in a small bowl
and beat in the reserved butter. Pour into the well
in the cornmeal mixture and stir gently until just
combined; do not overmix. Pour the mixture into
the hot skillet or dish.

4 Bake in the oven for 18–20 minutes, or until
the cornbread top is set and golden and a cake
tester or metal skewer comes out with just a few
crumbs attached when inserted into the middle.
Serve hot or warm, with butter.

Bacon & Caramelized

Onion Rolls

Makes 12 rolls

¹⁄₄ stick (2 tablespoons) butter
1 onion, finely chopped
1 teaspoon sugar
1 tablespoon vegetable oil, plus extra
 for brushing
4 ounces lean bacon, finely chopped

For the dough
4 cups bread flour, plus extra
 for dusting
1 teaspoon salt
2 teaspoons rapid rise yeast
1¹⁄₄ cups milk
1 egg, beaten

1 Melt the butter in a skillet. Add the onion and sugar and cook over a low heat for 25–30 minutes until the onion is deep golden. Remove and let cool.

2 Add the oil and bacon to the skillet and cook for 5 minutes. Mix the bacon with the onion and set aside until completely cold.

3 Put the flour in a large bowl and stir in the salt and yeast. Heat the milk until it is just hand hot and pour it into the flour. Add the egg, and onion and bacon, then mix together. Turn the dough out onto a well-floured board and knead for 10 minutes. Put the dough in a clean, oiled bowl, cover and let rise for 1 hour.

4 Punch down the dough with your fist to deflate, then divide it into 12 even-sized pieces. Knead each piece of dough for 2 minutes, then shape into a roll.

5 Preheat the oven to 425°F. Put the rolls on a large baking sheet and brush with oil. Let rise for another 20 minutes until doubled in size, then bake in the oven for 10–15 minutes until golden.

6 Remove the rolls from the oven and cover with a damp kitchen towel until cold—this will give the rolls a soft crust.

DESSERTS

- Berry Frozen Treats
- Mango Ice Cream
- Caramel Ice Cream
- Poached Pears with Maple Syrup & Pecans
- Pumpkin Pie
- Tropical Fruit Salad
- Meringues with Cream & Blueberries
- Spiced Baked Apples
- Sticky Toffee Pudding
- New England Blueberry Pancakes
- Double-crust Apple Pie
- Lychees with Orange & Ginger
- Chocolate Fondue
- Chocolate Mousse
- Chilled Tangerine & Lemon Mousse
- Baked Alaska Birthday Cake
- Apple Sauce Sundae
- Chocolate Chip Muffins
- Chocolate-covered Doughnuts
- Peanut Butter Brownies
- Apple Cake Bars
- Cherry Clafoutis
- Boston Cream Pie
- Stove-top Rice Pudding with Dried Fruit
- Summer Berry Shortcakes

CHAPTER SIX

DESSERTS

Berry Frozen Treats

Makes 6-8

2 cups water
2¼ cups sugar
1 pound mixed berries, fresh, canned, or frozen
Juice of 1 lime

Tip
Use any summer fruits to make these delicious, refreshing ice lollies. Try apricots, peaches, or raspberries.

1 Pour the water into a large saucepan and add the sugar. Bring to a boil and simmer for 2 minutes.

2 Remove the pan from the heat and let cool completely.

3 Put the berries in a blender and purée or mash well by hand. Add the lime juice and sugar syrup, and mix well.

4 Pour the mixture into frozen treat molds and leave to freeze overnight.

Mango Ice Cream

Serves 4

¾ cup sugar
3 egg yolks
1¼ cups milk
½ cup, plus 1 tablespoon heavy cream
2 ripe mangoes (total weight about
  ¾ pound)
2 tablespoons fresh orange juice
Fresh mango slices, to serve (optional)

1 Have ready a saucepan and a heatproof bowl that will fit on top of it. Put half the sugar in the bowl and add the egg yolks. Whisk until pale and thick. Half fill the pan with water, making sure the level is below that of the bowl when placed on top. Heat the water to simmering point.

2 Heat the milk and cream in a separate saucepan. When the mixture boils, stir it into the egg yolks. Place the bowl over the simmering water and stir continously until the mixture thickens to a custard that coats the back of a spoon. Let the custard cool, stirring it occasionally, then chill.

3 Peel the mangoes. Slice the flesh off each pit and put it in a blender or food processor. Process until smooth, then add the remaining sugar and orange juice. Process briefly to mix.

4 Stir the mango purée into the chilled custard. Churn the mixture in an ice cream maker. Alternatively, cover and freeze for 2 hours. Remove from the freezer and beat the mixture using a hand-held electric mixer or balloon whisk until smooth. Repeat freezing and whisking twice, then freeze until firm. The whisking during freezing prevents large ice crystals from forming and ensures that the ice cream is smooth.

5 Let the ice cream soften a little before serving in scoops in ice cream cones, or in bowls, with slices of fresh mango.

Caramel Ice Cream

Serves 6

½ cup sugar
About 3 tablespoons water
1¼ cups heavy cream
1 vanilla bean, split lengthwise or
   1 teaspoon pure vanilla extract
1¼ cups milk
5 egg yolks

1 Melt the sugar in a heavy-based saucepan with the water. As soon as the sugar has dissolved, increase the heat and boil until the sugar turns a very dark golden color—it is important to be bold here, or the ice cream will be too sweet. Carefully swirl the pan if the sugar isn't coloring evenly.

2 As soon as it is a dark mahogany color, remove from the heat, wait a minute, then pour on the cream, standing well back so you don't get splattered. When the bubbling subsides, stir until smooth.

3 Meanwhile, put the vanilla bean into a saucepan with the milk and bring to the boil, as before. Remove from the heat and set aside to infuse.

4 Beat the egg yolks until pale, then pour over the milk, discarding the vanilla pod. Return this mixture to a fresh saucepan and, stirring continuously with a wooden spoon, cook over gentle heat until thickened. Do not allow to boil or the egg will scramble. The custard is ready when the mixture coats the back of a wooden spoon without running off freely.

5 When cooked, add to the caramel and cream mixture, stirring until well blended.

6 Cover and freeze for 2 hours. Remove from the freezer and beat the mixture using a hand-held electric mixer or balloon whisk until smooth. Repeat freezing and whisking twice, then freeze until firm. The whisking during freezing prevents large ice crystals from forming and ensures that the ice cream is smooth.

7 Alternatively, use an ice cream machine, following the manufacturer's instructions.

Poached Pears

with Maple Syrup & Pecans

Serves 4

1 lemon
1 cup water
6 tablespoons pure maple syrup
1 cinnamon stick
4 firm pears
¼ cup light brown sugar
¼ stick (2 tablespoons) butter, diced
1¼ cups heavy cream
2 egg yolks
Chopped pecans, to decorate

1 Pare a long strip of zest from the lemon and put it in a large saucepan. Squeeze the lemon and set aside 1 tablespoon of the juice. Add the remaining juice to the pan, with the water and 2 tablespoons of the maple syrup. Add the cinnamon stick and heat, stirring gently all the time.

2 Peel the pears, leaving them whole. Add them to the syrup, carefully spoon it over them, then cover the pan. Poach the pears, basting them occasionally, until they are transparent and just tender, but still firm enough to hold their shape well. The timing will depend on the type of pears used, and their size, so check them frequently. When they are cooked, carefully transfer them to a dish and leave them to cool, spooning the syrup over from time to time. When cool, chill until ready to serve.

3 Meanwhile, put the brown sugar in a heavy-based saucepan and add the remaining 4 tablespoons maple syrup, the reserved lemon juice, and the butter. Heat gently, stirring, until the mixture is smooth. Remove the pan from the heat.

4 Heat the cream in a separate saucepan. When it is on the verge of boiling, pour it into the brown sugar mixture in a steady stream, stirring all the time.

5 Beat the egg yolks with 6 tablespoons of the cream mixture. Stir the mixture back into the pan and heat gently, stirring all the time until the sauce starts to thicken.

6 Drain the pears and add them to the maple sauce mixture to warm through gently. Serve the pears with the maple sauce spooned over and decorate with the chopped pecans.

Pumpkin Pie

Serves 4

1 pre-baked 12-inch pie crust
Cold light cream, to serve

For the filling
28-ounce can pumpkin purée
2 eggs, beaten
1/3 cup packed brown sugar
1 cup light corn syrup
1 cup heavy cream
2 teaspoons ground cinnamon
1 teaspoon ground ginger
1/2 teaspoon freshly grated nutmeg
1 teaspoon pure vanilla extract

1 Add the eggs, sugar, light corn syrup and heavy cream to the pumpkin purée and mix well. Stir in the spices and vanilla extract.

2 Spoon the mixture into the pie crust and bake in the oven for 30–35 minutes until the filling is firm to the touch. Serve warm with cold light cream.

Tropical Fruit Salad

Serves 4

1-inch piece fresh ginger, peeled and
   finely chopped
1³/₄ cups water
1 cup, plus 2 tablespoons sugar
1 star anise
1 stalk lemon grass
2 kaffir lime leaves
1 mango
1 papaya
2 firm pears
1 small melon, such as Ogen

1 Put the ginger, water, and sugar in a large saucepan. Add the star anise, lemon grass, and lime leaves. Bring to a boil then simmer quite fiercely for 20 minutes, or until the water has reduced and the liquid is quite syrupy. Remove the lime leaves and lemon grass. Let cool.

2 Cut the mango into cubes and put into a mixing bowl.

3 Halve the papaya lengthwise and scrape out the seeds. Peel carefully and cut into large cubes. Add to the mixing bowl.

4 Peel the pears and remove the core. Slice quite thickly and stir in with the other fruit.

5 Halve the melon and scrape out the seeds. Quarter and remove the flesh from the rind. Cut into ½-inch slices. Put in the mixing bowl. Pour the syrup over the fruit and serve chilled.

Meringues

with Cream & Blueberries

Serves 4

2 egg whites
Pinch of salt
6 tablespoons superfine sugar
Drop of pure vanilla extract
$^1/_2$ cup heavy cream
1 pint blueberries

1 Preheat the oven to 250°F. Line a baking sheet with parchment paper then set aside.

2 Using a hand-held electric mixer, beat the egg whites with the salt until stiff. Check this by lifting the beaters from the mixture and holding them upside down. If the tip of the egg white falls, the peak is soft. If it stands firm, it is stiff.

3 Add about half the sugar and whisk thoroughly. Keep whisking until the egg white no longer appears grainy and is very shiny and smooth. Add more sugar, about 1 tablespoon at a time, beating thoroughly between additions until all of it has been added. Add the vanilla extract. Keep beating until the mixture is smooth, thick, and glossy. If the sugar is not beaten in thoroughly enough, it will melt and leach out during cooking, making a very sticky mess.

4 Place 8 large spoonfuls of the mixture on to the prepared baking sheet, leaving plenty of space in between. Use the back of the spoon to make nice peaks on the tops. Transfer to the oven and cook for 1 hour, then switch off the oven and leave until cold. This will give the meringues a crisp outside and chewy, 'marshmallowy' inside. If you prefer them crisper, cook for 1$^1/_2$ hours then leave until cold.

5 Whip the cream until soft peaks form. Take one meringue and put a large spoonful of cream on the base and cover with mixed berries. Sandwich with another meringue and set aside. Repeat with all the meringues and all the cream. Serve immediately. The meringues will keep, without the added cream, in an airtight container for up to one week.

Spiced Baked Apples

Serves 4

6 large dessert apples
²/₃ stick (5 tablespoons) unsalted butter,
   softened
⅓ cup light brown sugar
1½ ounces fresh white bread crumbs
1 green cardamom pod
½ teaspoon ground cinnamon
¼ teaspoon freshly grated nutmeg
Pinch of saffron strands
Finely grated zest of ½ lemon
3 tablespoons golden raisins
3 tablespoons shelled and chopped
   pistachio nuts
1¼ cups apple cider
Cream, to serve

1 Preheat the oven to 400°F. Core the apples leaving them whole with the bottoms intact. Using a small sharp knife, make a horizontal cut around the middle of the apples—this will prevent the skin from bursting during cooking.

2 Cream the butter, sugar, and bread crumbs together in a medium mixing bowl. Crush the cardamom pods and remove the black seeds. Crush these using a mortar and pestle or with the back of

a spoon. Add to the butter mixture along with the cinnamon, nutmeg, saffron, and lemon zest. Mix everything together well. Stir in the golden raisins and pistachio nuts.

3 Stuff the mixture into the cored apples, stuffing piling any excess mixture on top of the apples. Transfer the apples to a ceramic or glass ovenproof dish large enough to hold them all with a little space in between. Pour the cider around the apples.

4 Transfer the dish to the preheated oven and bake for about 40-45 minutes until the apples are very tender.

5 Serve warm with the juices from the baking dish and some cream.

Sticky Toffee Pudding

Serves 2

1/3 stick (3 tablespoons) butter,
   softened, plus extra for greasing
1/4 cup brown sugar
1 egg, beaten
3/4 cup self-rising flour
1/3 cup chopped dates
2 tablespoons milk

For the sauce
1/3 cup brown sugar
1/2 cup heavy cream
1/3 stick (3 tablespoons) butter

Tip
This English pudding is
ideal with mascarpone or
crème fraîche. You could
substitute vanilla-flavored
prunes for the dates.

1 Grease a 1-quart pudding basin (deep heatproof bowl). Beat the butter and sugar together in a bowl until light and fluffy, then beat in the egg a little at a time. Fold in the flour, then stir in the dates and enough of the milk to give the mixture a soft, dropping consistency.

2 Spoon the mixture into the prepared bowl. Cut a round of parchment paper and a round of foil about 2 inches larger than the top of the bowl, and grease the bottom of the paper. Put both over the bowl and secure with string.

3 Put the bowl in a large saucepan and pour enough boiling water around the bowl, to come two-thirds of the way up the sides. Cover and simmer for 1–1½ hours until risen and springy when pressed. Check the water occasionally, topping up if necessary.

4 Put all the sauce ingredients in a small saucepan and heat gently, stirring, until combined. Simmer for 5 minutes, or until thickened. Turn the pudding out on to a plate and serve with the sauce.

New England Blueberry

Pancakes

Serves 4–6

1 cup, plus 2 tablespoons
  all-purpose flour
$1/2$ teaspoon baking powder
$1/2$ teaspoon baking soda
$1/4$ teaspoon salt
1 cup buttermilk
$3/4$ cup milk
1 tablespoon sugar or honey
$1/4$ stick (2 tablespoons) butter, melted
$1/2$ teaspoon vanilla extract
1 cup fresh blueberries
Melted butter or vegetable oil, for
  frying
Butter and pure maple syrup or honey,
  to serve

1 Combine the flour, baking powder, baking soda, and salt in a bowl and make a well in the middle.

2 Whisk the buttermilk, about ½ cup of the milk, the sugar or honey, melted butter, and vanilla extract together in another bowl. Pour into the well and, using a whisk or fork, stir gently until just combined with the dry mixture. If the batter is too thick, add a little more milk so that it can be poured. Do not overbeat—a few floury lumps do not matter. Gently fold in the blueberries.

3 Heat a large skillet or pancake griddle (preferably nonstick) over medium heat and brush with melted butter or vegetable oil. Drop the batter in small ladlefuls on to the hot surface and cook until the edges are set and the surface bubbles begin to break, about 1 minute.

4 Turn each pancake and cook until just golden underneath, about 30 seconds longer. Transfer to a baking tray and keep warm in a low oven until all the batter is cooked. Serve hot with butter and maple syrup or honey.

Double-crust Apple Pie

Serves 6–8

2 pounds cooking apples, peeled,
   cored, and sliced

1 tablespoon lemon juice

1 cup, plus 2 tablespoons sugar, plus
   extra for sprinkling

2 tablespoons flour

$\frac{1}{2}$–1 teaspoon ground cinnamon

Freshly grated nutmeg, to taste

1 tablespoon butter, for dotting

Vanilla ice cream, to serve (optional)

For the pie crust

$1\frac{2}{3}$ cups all-purpose flour, sifted, plus
   extra for dusting

1 teaspoon granulated sugar

$\frac{1}{2}$ teaspoon salt

1 stick (8 tablespoons) unsalted butter,
   cut into pieces, plus extra for greasing

3 tablespoons shortening, chilled

1 egg yolk

1 tablespoon lemon juice

4–6 tablespoons ice water

1 egg, lightly beaten, for glazing

1 To make the pie crust, put the flour, sugar, and salt into a food processor and pulse once or twice to blend. Sprinkle in the butter pieces and shortening and process for about 10 seconds until the mixture resembles coarse crumbs.

2 With the machine running, add the egg yolk, lemon juice, and the water little by little, until the dough begins to come together. Do not allow the dough to form a ball around the blade or it will be tough. Press a little of the dough between your thumb and forefinger; if it does not hold together, add a little more water.

3 Remove the dough and divide it in half. Flatten the pieces into rounds and wrap each in plastic wrap, then chill for 1–2 hours. Let soften slightly at room temperature before rolling.

4 Preheat the oven to 425°F. Lightly grease a 9-inch pie plate. Put the apples in a large bowl as they are prepared, sprinkle with the lemon juice and toss gently to combine. Mix the sugar, flour, cinnamon, and some freshly grated nutmeg together in a small bowl until combined. Sprinkle over the apples and toss to coat the fruit, then set aside.

5 Unwrap one dough round and place on a lightly floured surface. Roll out the dough from the middle towards the edge, turning it by a quarter turn as you roll to keep it in a round shape. The dough should be about ⅛ inch thick. Gently ease the

dough into the pie plate, pressing it in gently. Trim the excess, leaving ½ inch overlapping the edge. Brush the edge of the pastry with water and spoon the filling into the pie, mounding it slightly, then dot evenly with the butter.

6 Roll out the second dough round as before and place over the filling. With a sharp knife, cut a few slashes into the top to allow steam to escape. Trim the edge of the dough cover to the rim of the pie plate and turn the overhanging dough underneath up over the edge. Press to seal and crimp the edge. Brush with beaten egg. If you like, re-roll the trimmings and cut decorative leaves and fruits. Arrange on the pie and glaze again. Sprinkle with a little sugar.

7 Bake for about 25 minutes. Cover the edges of the pie with strips of foil to prevent them from over-browning and continue to bake for 20–25 minutes longer until the crust is set and golden and the filling is tender and bubbling.

8 Let the pie cool for at least 30 minutes before serving. Serve with vanilla ice cream.

Lychees
with Orange & Ginger

Serves 4

¹/₂ **cup granulated sugar**
¹/₄ **cup water**
2 oranges
16 lychees, peeled and pitted
2 pieces drained stem ginger, sliced
2 passion fruit

1 Heat the sugar and water in a small saucepan, stirring until the sugar has dissolved, then boil the syrup for 1 minute without stirring.

2 Pour the syrup into a serving bowl and set aside until cold. Peel the oranges and segment them, working over the bowl of syrup so that any juice is incorporated. Add the orange segments to the bowl with the lychees and ginger. Stir lightly to combine the ingredients.

3 Spoon into individual glass dishes. Cut the passion fruit in half and scoop the pulp over the fruit. Serve at once.

Chocolate Fondue

Serves 4

1½ cups heavy cream

1 cup milk

8 ounces bitersweet chocolate, roughly chopped

Marshmallows, strawberries, chopped bananas, cubes of brioche, and/or dates, for dipping

1 Pour the cream and milk into a saucepan or fondue bowl and bring to a boil. Turn off the heat and add the chocolate. Stir until the chocolate has melted and the mixture is completely smooth.

2 Serve the chocolate warm with a selection of marshmallows, fruits, and cakes or breads.

Tip

When melting chocolate, always break it into small pieces so that it melts evenly. If you are melting chocolate by itself, never melt it over direct heat—place it in a heat-proof bowl over a pan of hot water.

Chocolate Mousse

Serves 8

6½ ounces plain dark chocolate, 50 per cent cocoa solids

4 eggs, separated

¾ cup heavy cream, plus extra to serve

1 Break the chocolate into pieces in a small, heatproof bowl. Put the bowl over a saucepan of barely simmering water, ensuring that the bowl doesn't touch the water, and leave without stirring until the chocolate has melted. Remove from the heat and let cool for a few minutes.

2 Add 4 egg yolks and beat into the chocolate—it will thicken the mixture but not stiffen. If the mixture seems dry and stiff, the chocolate has been over-heated and you will need to start again.

3 Let the chocolate mixture cool for about 15 minutes.

4 Whisk the heavy cream until it holds soft peaks. Fold this into the chocolate.

5 Whisk 4 egg whites in a clean bowl until soft peaks form and fold into the chocolate mixture. Spoon into 8 small serving dishes, cover with plastic wrap and chill for about 2 hours before serving, with a little extra cream if desired.

Chilled Tangerine

& Lemon Mousse

Makes 6 small glasses

Grated zest and juice of 1 lemon
Grated zest of 2 tangerines and the
    juice of 4 tangerines
1 sachet powdered gelatin
4 eggs, separated
$\frac{1}{2}$ cup superfine sugar
$1\frac{1}{4}$ cups heavy cream

To decorate
Whipped cream
Pared lemon and tangerine zest

1 Put the fruit zest in a bowl. Measure the fruit juice—it should be no more than 1 cup. Pour the measured juice into a small saucepan and sprinkle the gelatin in. Let soak for 5 minutes, then heat gently without boiling until the gelatine has dissolved. Let cool.

2 Add the egg yolks and sugar to the fruit zest and whisk until the mixture is thick and creamy.

3 With clean beaters, whisk the egg whites in a clean bowl until stiff and whip the cream in another bowl until it forms soft peaks. Gently whisk the gelatine mixture into the yolks, then fold in the cream and finally the egg whites.

4 Spoon the mixture into glasses and chill for 3-4 hours until set. Decorate with whipped cream and lemon and mandarin zest.

Baked Alaska

Birthday Cake

Serves 6

8-inch soft sponge flan case

1½ cups raspberry jam

1 pint raspberries

4 egg whites

1 cup, plus 2 tablespoons granulated
   sugar

8 scoops vanilla or your favorite ice
   cream

Candles or sparklers, to decorate

1 Preheat the oven to 425°F. Spread the bottom of the flan case with the jam and arrange the raspberries on top.

2 Put the egg whites in a large clean bowl and whisk until stiff peaks form. Beat in the sugar, a spoonful at a time.

3 Put scoops of ice cream over the raspberries to cover. Spread the meringue mixture over the ice cream and sides of the sponge so everything is covered.

4 Bake in the oven for 8–10 minutes. Remove from the oven, decorate with birthday candles or sparklers, and serve immediately.

Applesauce Sundae

Serves 4

1½ pounds cooking apples, peeled, cored and chopped
¼ cup water
¾ cup granulated sugar
¾ stick (6½ tablespoons) butter
1½ cups fresh whole-wheat or rye bread crumbs
½ cup red currant jelly
½ cup heavy cream

Tip
You can add almost anything to a sundae. Try sprinkling flaked almonds, chopped or mini marshmallows on top.

1 Put the apples in a heavy-based saucepan with the water. Cover and cook over a medium heat until the apples are very soft, stirring frequently. Process them in a blender or food processor. Stir in 6 tablespoons of the sugar and leave until cold.

2 Melt the butter in a large skillet. Add the bread crumbs and remaining sugar and cook over low heat, shaking the pan frequently, until the crumbs have absorbed the butter and become crisp. Set the pan aside.

3 Warm the red currant jelly if necessary, so that it can be spooned. Layer the apple purée, jelly, and browned crumbs in 4 wine glasses, keeping back a little of the jelly for the decoration. Whip the cream until soft peaks form, then swirl it on top of each dessert. Drizzle the remaining red currant jelly over the cream and serve.

Chocolate Chip Muffins

Makes 10

- 3 cups all-purpose flour
- 3 tablespoons unsweetened cocoa powder
- 1 tablespoon baking powder
- $\frac{1}{2}$ teaspoon salt
- $\frac{1}{3}$ cup superfine sugar
- 4 ounces semisweet chocolate chips
- 2 eggs
- $\frac{1}{2}$ cup sunflower or light vegetable oil
- 1 cup milk
- 1 teaspoon pure vanilla extract

1 Preheat the oven to 400°F. Line 10 muffin pan cups with double paper liners. Sift the flour, cocoa powder, baking powder, and salt into a bowl. Sift again, then stir in the sugar and chocolate chips. Make a well in the middle.

2 Beat the eggs with the oil in another bowl until foamy. Gradually beat in the milk and vanilla extract. Pour into the well in the flour mixture, and stir until just combined.

3 Spoon the mixture into the paper liners. Bake for about 20 minutes until risen, well browned, and spongy. Leave to stand for about 10 minutes, then transfer to a wire rack to cool. Serve at room temperature.

Chocolate-covered

Doughnuts

Makes 8

2¹⁄₃ cups all-purpose flour
1 tablespoon rapid-rise dry yeast
Pinch of salt
¹⁄₄ cup granulated sugar
¹⁄₄ stick (2 tablespoons) butter, plus
    extra for greasing
²⁄₃ cup milk
2 egg yolks
Vegetable oil, for deep frying
2¹⁄₂ ounces semisweet or milk
    chocolate, broken into pieces
Chocolate jimmies, to decorate

1 Mix the flour in a bowl with the yeast and salt. Add the sugar, then rub in the butter until the mixture resembles fine bread crumbs.

2 Heat the milk in a saucepan until it is warm, then whisk in the egg yolks. Add the liquid to the flour mixture and mix to a soft dough. Cover with plastic wrap and set aside in a warm place for 1 hour or prove until the dough has doubled in bulk.

3 Grease a baking sheet. Punch down the dough and knead for 5–10 minutes on a well floured surface. Roll out the dough until ½ inch thick, and stamp out rounds with a plain biscuit cutter. Make a hole in the middle of each round with your finger. Put the doughnuts on the prepared baking sheet and let rise for at least 40 minutes or until doubled in size.

4 Heat the oil for deep-frying in a large deep saucepan to 375°F. Deep-fry the doughnuts one at a time for about 5 minutes, or until they are golden brown. Drain on paper towels and let cool.

5 Put the chocolate in a heatproof bowl set over a saucepan of simmering water. Heat until it has melted, then remove from the heat. Let cool slightly. Dip the rounded tops of the doughnuts in the melted chocolate, decorate with chocolate jimmies if you like, and let set.

Peanut Butter Brownies

Makes 12–16

6 ounces semisweet chocolate
2 sticks (16 tablespoons) butter
2¼ cups sugar
4 eggs, lightly beaten
2 teaspoons pure vanilla extract
⅓ cup all-purpose flour
½ teaspoon salt
6 ounces semisweet chocolate chips

For the peanut butter layer
1¼ cups smooth peanut butter
1 stick (8 tablespoons) butter, softened
3–5 tablespoons confectioners' sugar,
  plus extra for dusting
1 cup honey roasted peanuts or white
  chocolate chips

1 Mold a piece of aluminum foil in the bottom of an 8-inch square baking pan, pressing it into the corners and smoothing it out evenly.

2 Melt the chocolate and butter in a saucepan over a medium-low heat, stirring frequently, until smooth. Remove from the heat and add the sugar, then stir until the sugar dissolves. Beat in the eggs, then stir in the vanilla extract, flour, salt, and chocolate chips until just blended.

3 Spoon half the mixture into the pan and spread evenly into the corners. Freeze for 20 minutes until the surface is firm. Cover the remaining mixture and set aside at room temperature.

4 Preheat the oven to 350°F. Put the peanut butter and butter in a large bowl and, using a hand-held electric mixer, beat for about 2 minutes until smooth and creamy. Beat in the confectioners' sugar and peanuts or white chocolate chips. Drip tablespoonfuls of the peanut mixture over the chocolate layer, then gently spread it evenly to make a smooth layer. Cover with the remaining chocolate mixture in the same way.

5 Bake for 35 minutes, or until the surface is set. Leave in the pan to cool. Dust with a little confectioners' sugar and cut into squares or bars.

Apple Cake Bars

Serves 10–12

2¹/₂ sticks butter, plus extra for
  greasing
³/₄ pound tart cooking apples, peeled,
  cored, and thinly sliced
Juice of ¹/₂ lemon
1¹/₂ cups, plus 2 tablespoons sugar
3¹/₂ cups all-purpose flour, sifted
3 tablespoons baking powder
1¹/₂ teaspoons ground cinnamon
Grated zest of 1 lemon
6 eggs, beaten
3 tablespoons milk

For the topping
2 tablespoons coarse sugar
¹/₂ teaspoon ground cinnamon
6 tablespoons apricot jam, melted,
  to glaze

1 Preheat the oven to 350°F. Grease a 13 x 9 x 2-inch cake tin and line the bottom with parchment paper.

2 Toss the apple slices in the lemon juice. Cream the butter and sugar in a large mixing bowl until pale and fluffy. Sift in the flour, baking powder, and cinnamon. Add the lemon zest, eggs, and milk, and beat together until smooth.

3 Spoon half the mixture into the prepared pan. Top with half the apple slices, then the remaining cake mixture.

4 Arrange the remaining apple slices over the top and sprinkle with a mixture of coarse sugar and cinnamon.

5 Bake in the oven for 50–60 minutes until golden and firm to the touch. Let cool in the pan for 10 minutes them remove to a wire rack. Brush over the apricot jam, then let cool completely. Cut into bars to serve.

Cherry Clafoutis

Serves 4

½ stick (4 tablespoons) butter, melted,
  plus extra for greasing
2 tablespoons confectioners' sugar,
  plus extra for dusting
1 pound sweet cherries, pitted
1 cup self-rising flour
⅓ cup ground almonds
2 tablespoons sugar
⅔ cup milk
2 eggs

Tip
Clafoutis is a harvest dish from Limousin and Auvergne in France. It is a batter pudding filled with sweet black cherries —a substantial ending to a meal after a hard day in the fields.

1 Preheat the oven to 375°F. Grease a 9-inch shallow baking dish thoroughly and dust the bottom with the measured confectioners' sugar. Arrange the cherries on top.

2 Mix the flour, ground almonds, and sugar together in a bowl. Pour the melted butter into a pitcher and whisk in the milk and eggs.

3 Make a well in the center of the flour mixture and add the butter mixture. Stir well, gradually incorporating the flour, to make a smooth batter.

4 Pour the batter over the cherries and bake for 25 minutes. Let cool slightly, then dust with confectioners' sugar. Alternatively, run a knife around the rim of the dessert and invert it on to a flat serving platter. The top of the clafoutis (formerly the bottom) should be creamy and studded with cherries, while the rest of the mixture should have set to a sponge. Dust the top with confectioners' sugar.

Boston Cream Pie

Serves 8

Butter, for greasing
5 eggs
$^3/_4$ cup granulated sugar
1 cup, plus 2 tablespoons all-purpose
flour

For the filling
4 egg yolks
$^1/_4$ cup granulated sugar
$^1/_4$ cup cornstarch
2 teaspoons pure vanilla extract
2 cups milk
1$^1/_4$ cups heavy cream

1 Preheat the oven to 400°F. Grease and line the bottom of a 9-inch springform baking pan and a 10 x 7-inch shallow baking pan with parchment paper.

2 Put the eggs and sugar in a large heatproof bowl set over a saucepan of barely simmering water, and whisk until the mixture is pale and thick and holds a trail. Remove from the heat and whisk for a further 3–4 minutes, or until very light.

3 Sift the flour over the mixture and carefully fold in with a metal spoon. Spoon a very thin layer of the mixture over the bottom of the prepared rectangular baking pan to a depth slightly thicker than $^1/_8$ inch. Pour and scrape the rest of the mixture into the springform pan.

4 Bake both cakes for 12–15 minutes, or until light golden and firm; the cakes should spring back when lightly pressed with a finger. Let cool in the pans for 5 minutes, then turn out onto wire racks.

5 To make the filling, beat the egg yolks, sugar, cornstarch, vanilla extract, and 2 tablespoons milk together in a bowl. Heat the remaining milk in a saucepan to boiling point. Pour over the egg mixture, beating, then return to the pan and heat gently, stirring until thickened, but do not boil. Pour back into the bowl and cover with a piece of parchment paper. Let cool.

6 Cut the round cake horizontally into two layers and fit one back into the cleaned pan, cut side up. Trim the edges from the rectangular sponge, then cut into 1$^1/_4$-inch wide strips. Fit these around the side of the pan to make a shell.

7 Whip the cream in a chilled bowl until thick. Stir the cooled custard, and then fold in the cream. Pour into the cake shell. Lay the second cake on top, cut side up. Chill in the refrigerator overnight before serving.

Stove-top Rice Pudding
with Dried Fruit

Serves 4–6

1 quart milk
1 cup dried cherries, dried cranberries,
  dark or golden raisins, or a mixture
3–4 strips orange zest
1 cinnamon stick
1¼ cups short-grain rice, such as
  risotto rice
1 cup heavy cream
½ cup, plus 2 tablespoons sugar
1 teaspoon vanilla extract
¼ teaspoon salt
Cinnamon sugar, brown sugar or
  maple syrup, to serve
Whipped cream (optional)

Tip
It's best to use short grain rice for puddings and rice desserts as the grains swell and absorb the liquid to give a creamy consistency.

1 Put the milk, dried fruit, orange zest, and the cinnamon stick in a large, heavy-based saucepan and set over a medium heat. Bring to a simmer and stir in the rice.

2 Reduce the heat to low and cook, stirring frequently to avoid scorching, for about 20 minutes, or until the rice is tender and the mixture creamy.

3 Stir in the cream, sugar, vanilla extract, and salt and continue cooking for about 10 minutes longer, until the rice is completely tender and the mixture thick and creamy.

4 Pour the rice pudding into a large bowl and let cool to room temperature, stirring occasionally. Sprinkle with cinnamon sugar or brown sugar, or drizzle with maple syrup and serve with whipped cream, if desired.

Summer Berry

Shortcakes

Makes 8

2½ pints fresh ripe strawberries and other summer berries, hulled and sliced

2–3 tablespoons superfine sugar

1–2 tablespoons raspberry juice or 1 tablespoon orange juice

¾ stick (6 tablespoons) butter, diced, plus extra for greasing

8 ounces all-purpose flour, plus extra for dusting

2½ teaspoons baking powder

½ teaspoon salt

2 tablespoons granulated sugar, plus extra for sprinkling

1 cup heavy or whipping cream, whipped to soft peaks

Confectioners' sugar, for dusting

1 Put the berries in a large bowl and toss with the superfine sugar and fruit juice. Let stand until the juices begin to run, stirring occasionally.

2 Preheat the oven to 425°F and grease a baking sheet. Stir the flour, baking powder, salt, and granulated sugar together in a large bowl. Add the butter and, using a pastry blender or your fingertips, run it into the flour mixture until coarse crumbs form. Using a fork, lightly stir in all but 1 tablespoon of the cream, little by little, to make a soft dough.

3 Turn the dough out on to a lightly floured work surface and knead 6–8 times, until smooth. Pat or roll the dough into a rectangle about ½ inch thick. Using a round biscuit cutter, stamp out 8 rounds or, if you prefer, cut into 8 x 3-inch squares. Arrange 3 inches apart on the baking sheet. Brush the tops with the remaining cream and sprinkle with sugar.

4 Bake for about 10 minutes until set and the tops are pale golden. Transfer the shortcakes to a wire rack to cool.

5 Using a fork or serrated knife, split the shortcakes in half horizontally. Put the bottoms on 8 desserts plates and spoon the chilled whipped cream over them. Spoon over the berries. Put the shortcake tops on the berries and dust the shortcakes with confectioners' sugar.

Menu Ideas

Brunch

Chakchouka (p.129)
New England Blueberry Pancakes (p.226)

Grilled Cheese & Tomato Sandwiches
    with Bacon (p.54)
Green Bean & Mozzarella Salad (p.201)
Chocolate Chip Muffins (p.237)

Parsley & Leek Frittata (p.135)
Chocolate-covered Doughnuts (p.238)

Eggs Benedict (p.134)
Tropical Fruit Salad (p.221)

Lunch

Quick Mushroom Carbonara (p.59)
Apple Cake Bars (p.241)

Easy Burritos (p.75)
Berry Frozen Treats (p.214)

Bacon Cheeseburgers (p.68)
Chickpea & Tomato Salad (p.195)

Fish Stick Sandwiches
    with Mayonnaise (p.117)
Apple Sauce Sundae (p.236)

Chow Mein with Snow Peas (p.153)
Fava Beans with Prosciutto (p.108)

Italian Submarine Sandwiches (p.55)
Chilled Tangerine & Lemon Mousse (p.233)

New Potato & Crispy Bacon Salad (p.56)
Zucchini Bread (p.208)

Grapefruit, Shrimp & Avocado Salad (p.102)
Stove-top Rice Pudding with Dried Fruit
    (p.245)

Dinner Party Buffet

Chef's Salad (p.197)
Provençal Ratatouille (p.155)
Onion Quiche (p.139)
Tuna Melts (p.113)
New England Fishballs (p.120)
Peanut Butter Brownies (p.240)

Barbecue

Kansas City Pork Ribs (p.67)
Spicy Chicken Kabobs (p.20)
Grilled Corn-on-the-Cob with
    Flavored Butter (p.174)
Tropical Fruit Salad (p.221)

Dinner Party

New England Clam Chowder (p.94)
Rib Roast with Caramelized Shallots (p.76)
Duchesse Potatoes (p.166)
Cherry Clafoutis (p.243)

Smoked Trout Terrine
    with Cucumber Salad (p.121)
Roast Stuffed Chicken (p.34)
Luxury Mashed Potatoes (p.166)
Succotash (p.173)
Double-crust Apple Pie (p.228)

Home-smoked Salmon (p.92)
New England Potato Salad (p.172)
Beef & Onion Pies (p.70)
Brussels Sprouts
    with Sweet Potatoes (p.183)
Spiced Baked Apples (p.224)

Celebration Meal

Crab Louis (p.97)
Poached Whole Salmon (p.105)
Hot Vegetable Salad (p.184)
Baked Alaska Birthday Cake (p.235)

Caesar Salad (p.194)
Baked Ham (p.66)
Maple-baked Acorn Squash (p.189)
Latkes (p.171)
Boston Cream Pie (p.244)

Cheese Soufflé (p.131)
Roast Turkey with Sausage
    & Sage Stuffing (p.46)
Sweet Potato Casserole
    with Marshmallow Topping (p.176)
Carrots with Maple Syrup (p.182)
Pumpkin Pie (p.220)

Marinated Shrimps
    with Dill Mayonnaise (p.104)
Braised Lamb Shanks
    with Mirepoix Vegetables (p.80)
Leek & Potato Layer (p.169)
Sticky Toffee Pudding (p.225)

Dinner

Rice Vermicelli with Pork & Vegetables
    (p.63)
Braised Sugar Snaps with Lettuce (p.178)
Lychees with Orange & Ginger (p.229)

Patatas Bravas (p.167)
Spanish Pork with Tomatoes
    & Chorizo (p.64)
Spiced Zucchini (p.185)
Caramel Ice Cream (p.217)

Old-fashioned Meatloaf (p.78)
Potato Pancakes with Creamy Mushrooms
    (p.156)
Chocolate Mousse (p.232)

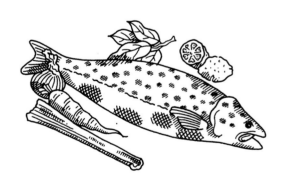

Roast Cod with Fried Gremolata
   Bread crumbs (p.119)
Pumpkin Couscous (p.146)
Chilled Tangerine & Lemon Mousse
   (p.233)

Honey-orange Chicken (p.32)
Risotto Primavera (p.142)
Mango Ice Cream (p.216)

Vegetarian Dinner
Roast Vegetable Lasagne (p.143)
Green Bean & Mozzarella Salad (p.201)
Poached Pears with Maple Syrup & Pecans
   (p.218)

Children's Sleepover Party
Warm Cheese & Smoked Chipotle Dip
   with Tortilla Chips (p.163)
Cheese & Tomato Pizza (p.127)
Southern Fried Chicken (p.24)
Panzanella (p.198)
Chocolate Fondue (p.230)

Picnic
Tortilla Wraps with Honey Roast Ham
   & Pepper Slaw (p.52)
Chicken Satay Skewers
   with Sweet Chile Sauce (p.23)
Classic Coleslaw (p.191)
Waldorf Salad (p.196)
Summer Berry Shortcakes (p.246)

Index

Acorn Squash, Maple-baked 189

Apple Cake Bars 241

Apple & Ginger Turkey Sandwiches 45

Apple Pie, Double-crust 228

Apples, Spiced Baked 224

Applesauce Sundae 236

Atlantic Spiced Salmon with New Potato & Spring Onion
Salad 93

Bacon: Bacon & Caramelized Onion Rolls 211

Bacon Cheeseburgers 69

Grilled Cheese & Tomato Sandwiches with Bacon 54

New Potato & Crispy Bacon Salad 57

Succotash 173

Baked Alaska Birthday Cake 235

Baked Ham 66

Baked Fish with Celeriac 116

Baked Lasagne 88

Baked Macaroni and Cheese 132

Baked Spinach Gnocchi 141

baking ingredients 14

Beans: Black Bean Chili 150

Cowboy Beans & Sausages 62

Fava Beans with Prosciutto 180

Green Bean & Mozzarella Salad 201

Mexican Pot Beans 190

Succotash 173

Beef: Baked Lasagne 88

Beef & Onion Pies 70

Beef Stew with Herb Dumplings 72

Beef Stew with Star Anise 79

Kofta 86

Pasta Shells filled with Bolognese 71

Old-fashioned Meatloaf 78

Rib Roast with Caramelized Shallots 76

Beer-battered Shrimps 100

Beet & Onion Mash 182

Beet Salad, Roast, with Oranges & Goat Cheese 126

Berry Frozen Treats 214

Black Bean Chili 150

Blueberry Pancakes, New England 226

Boston Cream Pie 244

bowls 10

Braised Fennel 177

Braised Lamb Shanks with Mirepoix Vegetables 81

Braised Sugar Snaps with Lettuce 178

Breads: Bacon & Caramelized Onion Rolls 211

Emmental & Roasted Corn Spoon Bread 207

Old-fashioned Cornbread 210

Zucchini Bread 208

Bream with Garlic & Coriander Butter 108

Broccoli Pilaf 205

Brownies, Peanut Butter 240

Brussels Sprouts with Sweet Potatoes 183

Burritos, Easy 75

Butternut Squash with Goat's Cheese 158

Cabbage Leaves, Stuffed 28

Caesar Salad 194

Caramel Ice Cream 217

Carrots with Maple Syrup 182

Cauliflower & Leek Patties 188

Chakchouka 129

Cheese: Baked Macaroni & Cheese 132

Butternut Squash with Goat Cheese 158

Cheese Fondue 130

Cheese Soufflé 131

Cheese & Tomato Pizza 127

Emmental & Roasted Corn Spoon Bread 207

Green Bean & Mozzarella Salad 201

Grilled Cheese & Tomato Sandwiches with Bacon 54

Roast Peppers with Mozzarella 154

Roasted Tomato & Goat Cheese Salad 200

Warm Cheese & Smoked Chipotle Dip 163

Chef's Salad 197
Cherry Clafoutis 243
Chicken: Chicken Hunter-style 29
    Chicken Kiev 33
    Chicken Satay Skewers 23
    Chicken & Sausage Gumbo 31
    Chicken Tikka 41
    Chicken & Vegetable Pie 38
    Chop Suey 60
    Club Sandwiches 26
    Easy Burritos 75
    Grilled Spiced Chicken 37
    Honey-Orange Chicken 32
    Lemon Chicken with Herb Tagliatelle 43
    Southern Fried Chicken 24
    Spiced Chicken Pilaf with Dried Fruit &
        Nuts 18
    Spicy Chicken Enchiladas 25
    Spicy Chicken Kabobs 20
    Spicy Chicken Sausages 44
    Spicy Peanut Chicken 40
    Stir-fried Chicken with Chile & Sweet Basil 21
    Stuffed Cabbage Leaves 28
    Traditional Roast Chicken 34
Chickpea & Tomato Salad 195
Chilled Tangerine & Lemon Mousse 233
Chips, Old-fashioned English 164
Chocolate Chip Muffins 237
Chocolate-covered Doughnuts 238
Chocolate Fondue 230
Chocolate Mousse 232
Chop Suey 60
Chow Mein with Snow Peas 153
Clam Chowder, New England 94
Classic Coleslaw 191
Club Sandwiches 26
Coconut Rice 206
Cod, Roast, with Fried Gremolata Bread crumbs 119
Coleslaw, Classic 191
Corn-on-the-Cob, Grilled, with Flavored Butter 174
Corn Salsa, Roasted 162
Cowboy Beans & Sausages 62

Crab Louis 97
Cream Pie, Boston 244
Crispy Fish Cakes 109
cutting boards 9–10

Double-crust Apple Pie 226
Duchesse Potatoes 166

Easy Burritos 75
Eggplant Parmigiana 144
Eggs: Chakchouka 129
    Egg-fried Rice 206
    Eggs Benedict 134
    Parsley & Leek Frittata 135
    Spanish Omelet 136
Emmental & Roasted Corn Spoon Bread 207
Enchiladas, Spicy Chicken 25

Fava Beans with Prosciutto 108
Fennel, Braised 177
Fish, Baked, with Celeriac 116
Fish Cakes, Crispy 109
Fish Caldine 99
Fish & Chips 96
Fish Finger Sandwiches with Mayonnaise 117
Fishballs, New England 120
Frittata, Parsley and Leek 135
Frozen Treats, Berry 214
Fruit Salad, Tropical 221

grains 11
Grapefruit, Shrimp & Avocado Salad 102
Green Bean & Mozzarella Salad 201
Green Curry 107
Grilled Cheese & Tomato Sandwiches with Bacon 54
Grilled Corn Cobs with Flavoured Butter 174
Grilled Spiced Chicken 37
Grilled Tuna with Warm Bean Salad 114

Ham: Baked Country Ham 66
    Italian Submarine Sandwiches 55
    Tortilla Wraps with Honey Roast Ham & Pepper Slaw 52

Harissa-coated Monkfish 122
health and safety 15
herbs 12–13
Home-smoked Salmon 92
Honey-orange Chicken 32
Hot Vegetable Salad 184

Ice Cream: Caramel 217
    Mango 216
Italian Submarine Sandwiches 55

Kansas City Pork Ribs 67
knives 8
Kofta 86

Lamb: Braised Lamb Shanks with Mirepoix Vegetables 81
    Kofta 86
    Lamb Meatballs with Buttermilk & Herb Dip 83
    Papaya Lamb Kabobs 84
    Roast Leg of Lamb 87
    Tagine with Prunes & Almonds 82
Latkes 171
Leek & Potato Layer 169
Lemon Chicken with Herb Tagliatelle 43
Lemon Herb Mayonnaise, Swordfish Kabobs with 98
Luxury Mashed Potatoes 166
Lychees with Orange & Ginger 229

Mango Ice Cream 216
Maple-baked Acorn Squash 189
Marinated Shrimps with Dill Mayonnaise 104
Meatballs: Lamb, with Buttermilk & Herb Dip 83
    Spicy Turkey 48
Meatloaf, Old-fashioned 78
Meringues with Cream & Blueberries 223
Mexican Pot Beans 190
Mixed Vegetable Curry 149
Monkfish, Harissa-coated 122
Mousse: Chilled Tangerine & Lemon 233
    Chocolate 232
Muffins, Chocolate Chip 237
Mushrooms: Potato Pancakes with Creamy Mushrooms 156

Quick Mushroom Carbonara 59
Stir-fried Greens with Shiitake Mushrooms 179

New England Blueberry Pancakes 226
New England Clam Chowder 94
New England Fishballs 120
New England Potato Salad 172
New Potato & Crispy Bacon Salad 57
nuts and seeds 13

oils 13
Old-fashioned Cornbread 210
Old-fashioned English Chips 164
Old-fashioned Meatloaf 78
Omelet, Spanish 136
Onion Quiche 139

pans 8–9
Panzanella 198
Papaya Lamb Kabobs 84
Parsley & Leek Frittata 135
Pasta: Baked Lasagne 88
    Baked Macaroni and Cheese 132
    Lemon Chicken with Herb Tagliatelle 43
    Pasta Shells filled with Bolognese 71
    Pasta with Fresh Tomato Sauce 140
    Quick Mushroom Carbonara 59
    Rice Vermicelli with Pork & Vegetables 63
    Roast Vegetable Lasagne 143
    Tomato Pasta with Italian Sausage & Lentils 58
    Tuna Noodle Casserole 112
pasta, types of 11
Patatas Bravas 167
Peanut Butter Brownies 240
Pears, Poached, with Maple Syrup & Pecans 218
Peppers, Roast, with Mozzarella 154
Poached Pears with Maple Syrup & Pecans 218
Poached Whole Salmon 105
Pork: Chop Suey 60
    Easy Burritos 75
    Kansas City Pork Ribs 67
    Rice Vermicelli with Pork & Vegetables 63

Spanish Pork with Tomatoes & Chorizo 64
Potatoes: Duchesse Potatoes 166
    Latkes 171
    Leek & Potato Layer 169
    Luxury Mashed Potatoes 166
    New England Potato Salad 172
    New Potato & Crispy Bacon Salad 57
    Old-fashioned English Chips 164
    Patatas Bravas 167
    Potato Pancakes with Creamy Mushrooms 156
Provençal Ratatouille 155
pulses 11
Pumpkin Couscous 146
Pumpkin Pie 220

Quiche, Onion 139
Quick Mushroom Carbonara 59

Ratatouille, Provençal 155
Rice: Broccoli Pilaf 205
    Coconut Rice 206
    Egg-fried Rice 206
    Rice Vermicelli with Pork & Vegetables 63
    Risotto Primavera 142
    Spiced Chicken Pilaf with Dried Fruit & Nuts 18
    Stir-fried Brown Rice & Vegetables 202
    Stove-top Rice Pudding with Dried Fruit 245
    Texas Pilaf 203
    Tomato Risotto 145
Rib Roast with Caramelized Shallots 76
Risotto Primavera 142
Roast Stuffed Chicken, 34
Roast Cod with Fried Gremolata Bread crumbs 119
Roast Leg of Lamb 87
Roast Peppers with Mozzarella 154
Roast Turkey with Sausage & Sage Stuffing 46
Roast Vegetable Lasagne 143
Roasted Beet Salad with Oranges & Goat Cheese 126
Roasted Corn Salsa 162
Roasted Tomato & Goat Cheese Salad 200
Roasted Vegetables with Pine Nuts & Parmesan 187

Salads: Caesar 194
    Chef's 197
    Chickpea & Tomato 195
    Classic Coleslaw
    Grapefruit, Shrimp & Avocado 102
    Green Bean & Mozzarella 201
    Hot Vegetable 184
    New England Potato 172
    New Potato & Crispy Bacon 57
    Roasted Beets, with Oranges & Goat Cheese 126
    Roasted Tomato & Goat Cheese 200
    Spinach and Mushroom, with Hot Bacon Dressing 192
    Waldorf 196
Salmon, Atlantic Spiced, with New Potato & Spring Onion Salad 93
Salmon, Home-smoked 92
Salmon, Poached Whole 105
Salmon, Sweet Chile 110
Sandwiches: Apple & Ginger Turkey 45
    Club 26
    Fish Stick, with Mayonnaise 117
    Grilled Cheese & Tomato, with Bacon 54
    Italian Submarine 55
seasonings 11–12
Shortcakes, Summer Berry 246
Shrimps: Beer-battered Shrimp 100
    Grapefruit, Shrimp & Avocado Salad 102
    Marinated Shrimps with Dill Mayonnaise 104
    Shrimp Jambalaya 103
    Green Curry 107
Smoked Trout Terrine with Cucumber Salad 121
Southern Fried Chicken 24
Spanish Omelet 136
Spanish Pork with Tomatoes & Chorizo 64
Spiced Baked Apples 224
Spiced Chicken Pilaf with Dried Fruit & Nuts 18
Spiced Courgettes 185
Spiced Grilled Sweet Potatoes 170
spices 13
Spicy Chicken Enchiladas 25
Spicy Chicken Kabobs 20
Spicy Chicken Sausages 44

Spicy Peanut Chicken 40
Spicy Turkey Meatballs 48
Spinach Gnocchi, Baked 141
Spinach & Mushroom Salad with Hot Bacon
    Dressing 192
Spinach with Paneer 151
Spinach Roulade 157
Sticky Toffee Pudding 225
Stir-fried Brown Rice & Vegetables 202
Stir-fried Chicken with Chile & Sweet Basil 21
Stir-fried Greens with Shiitake Mushrooms 179
Stove-top Rice Pudding with Dried Fruit 245
Stuffed Cabbage Leaves 28
Succotash 173
Sugar Snaps, Braised, with Lettuce 178
Summer Berry Shortcakes 246
Sweet Potato Casserole with Marshmallow Topping 176
Sweet Potatoes, Spiced Grilled 170
Swordfish Kabobs with Lemon Herb Mayonnaise 98

Tagine with Prunes & Almonds 82
Tangerine & Lemon Mousse, Chilled 233
Texas Pilaf 203
Tomato & Goat Cheese Salad, Roasted 200
Tomato Pasta with Italian Sausage & Lentils 58
Tomato Risotto 145
Tomato Salsa 162

Tomato Sauce, Fresh, Pasta with 140
Tortilla Wraps with Honey Roast Ham & Pepper Slaw 52
Tropical Fruit Salad 221
Trout Terrine, Smoked, with Cucumber Salad 121
Tuna, Grilled, with Warm Bean Salad 114
Tuna Melts 113
Tuna Noodle Casserole 112
Turkey Meatballs, Spicy 48
Turkey, Roast, with Sausage & Sage Stuffing 46
Turkey Sandwiches, Apple & Ginger 45
Turkey-stuffed Peppers 49

Vegetable Curry, Mixed 149
Vegetable Lasagne, Roast 143
Vegetables, Roasted, with Pine Nuts & Parmesan 187
Vegetable Stir-fry 148

Waldorf Salad 196
Warm Cheese & Smoked Chipotle Dip with Tortilla Chips 163
whisks 10

Zucchini Bread 208
Zucchini, Spiced 185